Spiritual Science of Success

Elevate Your Mind Master Your Life

Ken Viñales

For information contact:

TheRareFew.com

@WiseKen777 - Instagram

@WiseKen777 - Twitter

ISBN: 978-0-9994018-6-6

First Edition: November 2020

Authors Note

I am on my third book. When this book was initially completed, it was a week before my 24th Birthday. 100 original author copies were signed and released. I began writing to help people learn their true power. Lives have already been changed by my words. My goal before I leave this earth is to write and publish 30 books. These books are independently created and self-published. There is not a team or funding behind me, only passion, vision, and dedication. I am not sure what the next 27 books will be about. I just know something is always hit when you aim and shoot. Lives have been transformed, long after I have died by these words. These words have traveled through generations as inspiration. Thank you for helping me make this vision come true.

Contents

Part 1
Elite Secrets

Why do those who excel in their field stand out? "Those" in this passage will be referred to as the elite. To be elite requires an understanding of the mind that is spiritual and scientific. Science questions everything unless there is supporting evidence, deeming the subject as a fact. Spirituality, on the other hand, requires blind faith. The invisible energy that connects you to this universe's creator is a belief based on faith.

Some scientists do not believe in spirituality, but the truth is that everything requires the use of spiritual forces. Without spirituality, the reality that you live in would not be in existence. Indeed, consciousness or God cannot be quantified, but that is why both fields' interplay produces success. How can you develop these abilities?

The simple truth is that geniuses are created consciously, although many are conditioned unconsciously. Furthermore, highly skilled individuals apply psychological laws to their life, knowingly and unknowingly. In other words, there is an exact way to create success in any field if the interplay between the spiritual and scientific world is understood. You will learn a specific science, a set of laws that will enable you to tap into the highest energy and intelligence source. How is this information different than something you have come across before?

This book will provide you with breakthrough psychological techniques to master your life and elevate your mind. The information presented was gathered and organized by an expert in the field of psychology and sociology. By tapping into this universal intelligence source, you will learn how to direct and control energy at the highest intensity. The truth is that your human brain is easy to program and very similar to a computer.

Information enters your mind as data. Data is processed by the mind, stored for later use, or materialized. The material form of data is known as an experience. The close relationship between a computer and the human mind is what allows individuals to become elite. Your ability to acquire knowledge, learn skills, and create wisdom, determines the levels you can reach in this material world. To master skills, there must be a conversion, internally, of information into organized energy.

When 10,000 hours of organized energy is invested in a specific field, it opens the door for mastery. Understand now, the elites invest much more than 10,000 hours. That is the generic number. It will not be possible to master dozens of skills in your life, which is why this next key is vital to know. Find one natural talent, then implant relevant information through encoding, which will be explained more in part four.

The process that it takes to master one skill will make it easier for you to become adept at other crafts. An array of skills that can be unified makes life easier to navigate. Exposure will reveal how to get what you need and from whom you need to absorb information. If you can master one skill, it will open up doors in other areas of life.

The secret to skill mastery is information conversion through data consumption and application. Information can be obtained through many different channels. Intelligence dictates the capacity in which you can consume a stimulus, then transform that stimulus into a real-life experience. Hence, data conversion, absorbing information to create experiences, so wisdom is extracted. When your mind takes in information, it is received as data. Just because a person consumes data does not mean they know how to yield wisdom and advance in life.

The current generation has access to something called the internet. The internet is something that people in past eras were not able to imagine. It is a luxury to have platforms like Google and YouTube, where information can be gathered in seconds—coming back to the point.

4

Two people can have the same opportunities and resources, but the data is converted differently in each person's mind, dictating their perception of reality.

The intelligent person understands how to transform mental data, into extractable experiences, for future development. When you create an experience, what you take from that is wisdom. Knowledge consumption can be seen as a door, a door that births wisdom. When information is applied to the physical world, wisdom is born.

Wisdom is essential because knowledge or information without experience is philosophy. On the flip side, experience without knowledge is ignorance. The interplay between the two produces wisdom. Once the mind is wired for a belief, habit, or direction, it is more than likely going to transpire into the real world. As time goes on, your mind will learn how to transform data into an awakening experience for future advancement.

Take a moment to think back to the beginning days of life. Upon entering this world, each human is a blank slate. There are no experiences, information, or knowledge of the world. A lack of understanding creates dependency. The environment a child is conditioned in will have an enormous impact on their reality and future.

Over time, information entered your mind as data was stored as an experience, fact, idea, or lesson and helped you interact with the world. The reality around you is created through your experiences. Have you taken the time to study them? Your mind projects the beliefs you have adopted onto the world. Your energy and habits will attract a particular life to you, which you are currently living in.

The environment you were raised in does most of the early mental conditioning, for those form your beliefs on love, self-esteem, discipline, and many habits ingrained in you. The purpose of this manuscript is to take you behind the scenes of your mind. You will be given an exact science, set of laws, and formula to reconstruct your mind. If you are good, this will make you great. If you are great, it will turn you into a legend.

What about those who are lost? The average? If this information becomes organized knowledge, there will be no limitation in this world for you. The result will be riches. When success is studied, down to the core, what will be found is that it begins with one's mind, your mind. These laws and practices must be understood before they can be obeyed.

Many desire success. Many people speak of success. Many claim success. The question arises when life transpires, and only a small percentage of people can reach elite levels. While money, status, and power all play a role, the most important key is the master, in other words, your mind.

Those who reach elite levels have a keen connection with universal intelligence. The same universal intelligence that you are connecting with now. There is nothing different from how the mind functions, from person to person, at the primary level. What varies is the capacity of understanding that each individual has for their brain and mind. Once the mind is understood, it makes it easy to program your brain.

The mind is unique because of its ability to absorb data. Think about the number of things that do not require thought. When is the last time it required thought to walk, speak, or see? All of these basic functions activate neurons inside of your brain. What are neurons?

Neurons are cells. These cells transmit energy and information from your brain to other areas of the brain. Data is also transported throughout your body through the nervous system. Why is this important to understand? Each function previously stated requires some type of brain activity, but the sight of that is unavailable.

Neurons are vehicles of data that shape your reality through transportation. How do these neurons work?

When an idea, action, or emotion is evoked, the effect is a neuron firing in the brain. Information serves as a stimulus for your mind, which can create beliefs, subconsciously instilling habits. Humans are subconscious animals. Humans are lazy, which is why you rely on the subconscious mind so much.

Imagine a piece of clay that is used for pottery. It starts as just a block or ball of clay. As the potter molds the clay, it begins to form into a vessel. Once the vessel is constructed, it is fired at high temperatures to give it a hard, durable shape, which is the same thing that happens to your brain through exposure and repetition.

Now imagine what happens if the vessel is dropped after it crystallizes. Your mind should have envisioned the shattering of a vase. In this example, the vase represents the process that your mind undergoes when it receives a powerful message or sign. This information entered your life for a reason, and the result will be a complete halt of your reality. The result will lead to a rapid increase in mental, spiritual, and emotional growth.

When the mind has a shift, in reality, a collection of things happen. The first is already underway, which begins with questioning. Questions act as a key because it creates openings that were once non-existent. What does that mean? When you ask yourself why your beliefs will begin to take on a different meaning. Subconsciously you will search for answers to questions never considered. Answers can only be found within.

Why are you where you are today? Why do you follow the religion that you believe in? Why do you love the way you love? Why do you make the amount of money that you do? Why do you want the things you want?

The "why" phase is the shattering phase because it sends your mind on a lifelong journey. An unconscious force will draw information to you. New information allows for the molding of your brain. As you uncover more details, experiences will materialize. Once your knowledge becomes an experience, the reshaping process initiates.

Your mind is like the potter, and your brain is the clay. Your brain is remarkably plastic and has the capability of being molded. Now substitute your hands for your words, thoughts, and environment. These are examples of what affects the clay; in other words, the programming of your brain. Beliefs and habits take life through repetition and exposure. Once it becomes a part of your subconscious mind, less thought is required, and the odds of a reversal are slim.

Your mind is separate from your brain, meaning it cannot be seen nor quantified. Unlike the brain, which is an organ, the mind has no true limitations. There is a unique similarity with the entire universe. What does this mean? Years of research has been done on this thing called the universe. The universe as a whole entity is impossible to imagine in the mind.

In the invisible world of thought, the only limitation is whatever you allow the limit to be. The world's elites understand the spiritual and can tap into some of the highest dimensions of thought through science. In the invisible world exists emotions, beliefs, energy, frequency, and consciousness. Deduce the invisible world down to an atom in your brain, and there will be a shift.

The same atoms that created this universe from nothingness are the same atoms that make up your organs. At the basic level, atoms consist of energy, the foundation of the universe. Your environment is nothing more than information for your mind to encode into your brain, which will be explained more in parts four and five. An essential part of encoding is attentional capture. Without attentional capture, it is more challenging to learn something.

What will empower you is the acquisition of wisdom through high information intake, followed by application. The activation of neurons transfers into your brain. When you think, act, or spend time in an environment, neurons activating transmit information.

The spiritual world is essential to understand because of the oneness that you share with it. The scientific world is vital to understand because it reveals formulas and laws that bind specific outcomes to nature. Both are more powerful together because it combines the laws of nature with the laws of the universe. What this does is provide you with a way to control reality.

When beginning a journey, there must be an envisioned destination; write it down, for which your mind will find a direction. Whatever you decided upon is what will appear in your outside reality. For this form of thinking to come to life, you must make a sacrifice. One sacrifice may be ceasing all preconceived notions or beliefs. For you to understand the mind of the elite, you must adopt the mentality of the elite.

Throughout this manuscript, facts and philosophies will be presented. This new perspective will empower you with information and knowledge. People are blind to many things; sometimes, it can be their greatness. You can encode greatness into your mind, like installing software onto a computer. You are subconsciously programmed everywhere you turn. If you do enough studying, your mind will begin to seek more truth and ask more questions.

You have been programmed. Whether you have taken the time to understand that fact or not, it is true. The real power comes when you encode intelligence for exponential growth. Since birth, your brain and mind have been under the influence of everything around you beyond your control. The environment you live in, the media you consume, the people you spend time with all shape your brain. Those variables will determine who you become, what you feel, how you think, and what you see.

As a human, you will be programmed, so why not learn how to do it yourself? Through this course, you will develop every tool that you need to experience the success you envision. Knowledge empowers you, only if you are knowledgeable enough to apply it. As you consume more relevant knowledge, a change in mind will persist. The science presented has been extracted from research and some elite individuals' minds from various fields.

From a broad perspective, the encoding begins at an early age. Some are unaware of this, as well as many other things. Take a moment to think about some of the things you may have believed in as a child. Were you ever excited about Santa Claus? How about putting your tooth under a pillow? What about the fantasies that you had during your adolescent years.

What has changed from then until now? Do you still believe in the same things? Do you still have the same excitement for specific ideas? The answer will reveal a change in your mind, but what was the cause of the change? The underlying catalyst for change will be experiencing different things. When your mind becomes aware of something it was not before, a transformation is initiated.

You cannot change what you are unaware of, which is the first step. Enhance your perspective. Ask more questions. Think about why things are the way they are. What's so interesting about the human mind is the constant activity. Even when you are not aware, your mind is always working and scanning the environment.

For instance, are you controlling the pumping of your heart? The subconscious mind is in control of your survival. In other words, your subconscious mind is always scanning and absorbing the environment. Your conscious mind is your identity. The conscious mind is what allows you to focus and produce energy.

Your mind feeds off of its surroundings. The environment is food to your mind. What your mind consumes will affect the lens that perceives life. People from similar areas have similar forms of communication, ways of life, and sources of entertainment. That truth should be an indicator of how the mind absorbs its natural surroundings.

Greatness begins in the mind. The elite has a unique understanding of science, combing it with the spiritual realm. You will learn the secret to developing this elite mindset. The *Spiritual Science of Success* will help you see how close you are to the top. The first step is enhancing your perspective.

New information can be hard to dissect. When exposed to new ideas, it can create an internal shock or confusion. Knowledge is powerful, but it is not equal to power. Do not get the cliché confused with real life. Organized knowledge is power when directed precisely. If information is not applied to create an experience, then it lies in the mind, useless. Internal data must become material wisdom.

Now that you are internalizing this information, it will be vital to adopt the laws and practices. Perception will play a large role. Without an open mind, it will be difficult to understand. Lack of understanding will only make the application process more confusing. In short, many practical tools will be provided.

The greater your perspective, the more aware you will become. The way to increase perception is through breaks of reflection. Reflection will allow your mind to observe from an outside point of view. Old experiences will begin connecting themselves to new information, which in turn will produce wisdom.

It is impossible to predict every event in life, but you can better grasp what happens to you if you can slow life down. In other words, with higher awareness, you will be allowed to alter outcomes with a more precise perception. This manuscript will reveal to you the secret science, which will elevate your mind and spirit.

This manuscript will expose you to research that began centuries ago. These words were not written for entertainment, rather for enlightenment. You must be an individual who obsesses over success. You must want to live your life with purpose. Last, you must value growth and accountability. No matter who you are or where you are, there is always more you can learn.

Billionaires, athletes, scientists, actors, investors, and many more have used the information presented. If you feel that you cannot benefit from what is being shared, you will not gain from what is being taught. The wise man knows he knows nothing at all. As you go deeper, your mind will begin to form new ideas while building on the existing thoughts. Welcome to the spiritual science of success.

Part 2

Mind Power

To desire success is a natural emotion. Anyone with moderate levels of ambition will want to live their version of a dream life. The reality of dreams, or even success, is that only a small percentage of the population gets to the other side of the fence. What separates one individual from another? How will you rise above everyone else in your chosen field to reach the levels you desire?

In a world with social media, success seems so tangible. Everywhere you scroll, someone is living their "dream" life. Every day someone or something new is going viral. Most of you will wonder what it is like to have millions of followers, dollars, or both. There will be some who trade in their morals for fame and money. Then you will have those who receive it, without ever wanting it.

Before diving into the psychology, take a moment to analyze the primary source of media in this modern era. With the rise of social media, fame and success seem to be the same. Beyond fame and success, the dream life seems to be more tangible. Many people mention manifestation and speaking things into existence, but what is that?

Although there are some truths to those beliefs, there must be some context to that information.

With the heavy influence of social media on world trends and business exposure, it can seem impossible to reach success without it. That thought alone can cause people to forget the bigger picture. At the root, success remains the same; no matter what period, no matter what trend, these laws and practices will always help you prevail. A seed must be planted and nurtured continuously for a flower to grow.

What you must take from this manuscript is that all humans are, in a way, heavily influenced psychologically. The question can be, where's the proof? Or the question can be, well, how do you stop it? What you need to understand is that it cannot be stopped. Everything you consume influences you. The media you consume, the environment you live in, and your information source all play a substantial role in who you are.

Mental encoding is relatively easy to accomplish. By altering a few variables, a person can be under the influence of someone or something without knowledge or consent. Many people live their life blind. They wake up, go to work, eat, sleep, then repeat. Ten percent of people control most of the world, while the other ninety percent are at the mercy of the few.

If you want to join the ten percent, the elite, their mindset must be adopted. The foundation of a correct mindset is organized thought. There are people with hustle, ideas, ambition, and information, but something they lack is organized thought control, which you will learn. This will form the foundation of power. Without power, success will not be possible.

The media's and society's influence over you goes much deeper than anything you can see. There is no need to become irrational about the control those at the top have over you and society. What can be gained is knowledge. This philosophy has been used for generations. While there is no way to stop what is happening to you, there is a way to take back some control. You can apply the same method to the ideas and beliefs of your own. The result will produce any outcome you want.

The information that you consume will slowly begin to show itself throughout your reality. New ideas will sprout. New emotions will be unlocked, and your vision will become more precise. You have a chance to enter this new world. If you have already entered this world, then to explore parts of the world you may have never seen.

This new world, this mental world, is one that can be hard to understand. Not only hard to understand, but if understood, it can be hard to implement. Success is not easily attainable but can easily be obtained by any individual. Many people talk about success; only a few ever get to experience it.

You live in the digital age, where people are building followings online and creating e-Commerce businesses. No matter what a person believes success to be or how to reach it, one thing cannot be denied. Success, no matter what the endeavor, begins with a person's mindset. Along with mindset, power is vital to understand.

Without power, you will not be able to reach elite levels. Power can be created through many channels. The energy that you will learn to possess will unleash the power of your mind. To develop power, you must first understand it at a basic level. You will also develop the ability to create energy at your own will, but you will also learn how to direct it. The mind that becomes a unit of power transforms the world into a canvas.

Think of yourself as an artist, with paint being the thoughts and the world being your canvas. The power that you learn, using energy to orchestrate your thoughts, will create a matching reality of whatever you envision. As you develop more strength, it will become easier to move groups of people and shift reality. Take a look at power from a broad perspective. What is it?

When you organize your energy, power is born. What does that mean? Imagine the sun under a magnifying glass. Non-directed Sun rays have power, but what happens when placed under a magnifying glass? The Sun's rays are intensified, which can make the effect more dangerous. Now translate the same concept to thinking.

Merely thinking about something exerts energy into the universe. A single thought activates neurons inside of your brain. Many people spend most of their time engaged in purposeless thought, not organized or directed. The basic definition of power is organized energy or effort. When someone sits around and wastes thoughts, engages in negative thinking, or indulges in excessive entertainment, their thoughts are not organized on something definite. Their thoughts can be considered scattered or negatively charged, meaning that a series of adverse events will transpire.

It's as if society is taught to believe that the universe is apart from them. The universe is nothing more than a system of energy organized into different species, planets, and other concepts, that exist in your reality. It is taught that space is somewhere up above, along with the sun, stars, moon, and other planets throughout the school system. The saying, shoot for the moon, is an analogy that encourages you to aim high.

Many cliché sayings are accepted as real, without proper thought or question. It is a fact that one should aim high, strive for big goals, and want better. The misconception, rather ignorance of the unity of the universe, prohibits them from reaching elite levels. Ten percent of the world control the other 90 percent. While it may not be right and eventually lead to an uprising, there is an innate ability for you to experience a higher dimension of thought.

In the spiritual world, there is no separation between you and the entire universe. What does that mean? Currently, you are in the physical world. In the last decade, another world has been created. The world of social media is a virtual world. So what is the spiritual world, and how does it affect you?

When you think a thought, there is no visible detection. Thoughts activate something in the brain called a neuron. A neuron's purpose is to transfer energy from different areas of the brain and body through the nervous system. Your nervous system acts with the sole purpose of survival. To think a thought requires consciousness, which is a product of the brain, but not limited to the brain because it exists in the mind.

When you learn how to command the present moment, it puts you on the same frequency as the entire universe. This means that power can flow through you and from you. The power exists within. In the present moment, it is possible to use conscious energy to implant beliefs, visions, habits, and information; this will be discussed more in part five.

If the universe could come into creation from nothingness, then there should be no excuse for you. Not only does the universe live within your mind, but your mind also has the entire world as a canvas. The elites use this spiritual science of success to get ahead in all areas of life, from sports to finance, politics, and much more. Nothing is limiting you once these laws are internalized.

A law is something that is bound by force. Specific outcomes will always transpire in nature because of the strong connection to the universe. The law of divine-oneness states precisely what you are. The definition of divine means god or godlike. Oneness means unified. All life force comes from one source, meaning everyone is connected to the highest power.

Life doesn't exist tomorrow or yesterday. The past or future is not real; instead, they are concepts. Practicing present moment awareness unifies you with the highest source of energy. The result of this can be many things, such as peace, clarity, and direction. During the present moment, one can practice meditating or coming into the present.

In the present moment, there is no thought. During the present moment, there is no awareness of emotion. What this means is that you are just experiencing the divine energy or life in its entirety. Elites practice meditation for many reasons. Like many other sections of the body, the brain, mind, tandem is a muscle.

Practicing present moment awareness will translate to the mastery of other skills. Why is that? Studies show that meditation increases creative ability, which is necessary for manifesting in the physical world. Another finding is that areas that are related to recall, memory, and learning are active during the process of meditating.

When you learn how to command energy while performing a task, it allows you to master the skill, which will be discussed more in part four. Mastery is the ability to perform a skill at a high level, with little conscious thought or effort. To become elite, it is a must to know the science of mental encoding. The mind is similar to a computer, in the sense that programs are downloaded, then initiated.

As a human, there are laws of nature that also rule over you. The laws of nature are essential to understand because they scientifically explain how you interact and react to society and the environment. It is impossible to be separate from nature as a human, and nature results from the universal energy. In short, there are many layers to your functioning, requiring understanding for power to be obtained.

Systematic thought can be considered the basis of power. When your thoughts are scattered, you are powerless. When your thoughts are negative, your actions are destructive rather than constructive. The inability to focus for long periods separates those at the bottom and top. Meditation is a practice that helps people increase focus and mental energy.

The modern era has resulted in a lack of attention. Many things have become available instantly. What that has created is a higher need for instant gratification, the desire to experience pleasure without delay. Instead of investing years of time and focus, people would rather accomplish goals immediately. The result has been difficulty to remain focused or retain energy.

Being able to scroll through timelines, switch entertainment instantly, going from Instagram to YouTube, then Twitter created a change in human psychology. Then, companies like Amazon can deliver a product to your house in 24 hours or less. Society is forgetting what it is like to wait.

The amount of time people have to wait is slowly becoming non-existent, increasing the need for instant gratification. Instant gratification has become more of a driving force than the process itself. What you are living through is an increase in the need for immediacy amongst society. The blind are being led on a never-ending roller coaster. Humanity, as a whole, is developing a habit of not waiting for things.

Habits are powerful because they begin to show in all areas of life. People transmute their desire for immediacy onto success. Over time, their reality will get shattered over and over again because of one reason. Success is not something that comes quickly, for if it does, you should engage with caution. Anything received too fast has the possibility of exiting as fast, if not quicker.

People who fall into the trap of instant gratification are deemed to come up short. Human thought is easy to manipulate, which is often overlooked. All of what you think, see, or feel is heavily influenced by the outside world, society, and the media. To gain more control, you must understand power, your power. The way you organize facts and knowledge determines the rate at which your mind will become a unit of force.

Organized thought can be seen all across the world and at different intensities. It can be great or awful. Think about magnified sun rays. Do some research on Fortune 500 companies. Enter the lives of those who retain wealth. Have you taken the time to study the mind and process of those who are successful?

What you will quickly internalize is the power of harmony. To enter the present moment, focus your thoughts and organize your energy with purpose. The more you enter this state of being, the benefits will be more incredible. When you are not guided by intelligence or truth, organized energy can be dangerous. The danger comes because it can lead you down a path of destruction. Power lives on a spectrum, as well as energy; that is why the two are closely related.

There is a positive spectrum, where good is produced and also where construction lives. On the opposite side of the spectrum, negative experiences are born, and destruction rules. Self-awareness enhances your ability to control this spectrum. Many people are unaware of the effects. Once your thoughts become the subject of another person's influence, your power is ceased.

Human thought is the highest, when organized, form of energy known to man. Your mind is nothing more than a mass of motivating forces that grow from your daily habit. Any idea that is deliberately fixed in the mind, through suggestion, is guaranteed to influence your actions, reality, and future. Your mind reacts to any suggestion that you focus on or implant.

The result of organized thought will cause you to indulge in acts that conform around the planted belief or idea. Your power is your ability to organize your thoughts around abundant ideas. The goal is to exert your energy with purpose. Once you form the habit of thinking of abundance and moving with a definite purpose, the material evidence will appear.

The downfall of many begins with their thought pattern. There are times where your thoughts may seem to have control, but your will-power allows for dictatorship. Why is thought control so necessary? Take a moment to imagine a hot summer day. It is 85 degrees outside, with no clouds or a chance of rain. The sun can be felt, but what happens if you take a magnifying glass and place it under the sun at the right angle?

Thought control is the first step to enhancing your inner mind power. Once you learn how to control your thoughts fully, the energy you exert will become more precise. The magnification of sun rays allows for burning at high temperatures. As you learn to control your thoughts, you will have more power to manifest into the physical world. How do you get to this point?

It is easy to get lost in your thoughts. The reason this happens is due to a lack of understanding. Thoughts themselves can be studied, but that is not always acknowledged. Thought control requires understanding and awareness. Awareness is vital for the completion of your process. In fact, without awareness, it will be impossible to gain full control.

Throughout life, your mind will consume many things. To be more specific, you will retain many facts and much information. When developing the correct mindset, you must learn how to precisely separate facts from mere information. There is a lot of information in this world, but not everything is derived from fact, which is vital to comprehend.

Beyond comprehension, you must make accurately separating fact from information a habit. Information may be accurate or factual but will not always be relevant to your situation. Organize facts into separate categories, relevant and irrelevant. You may encounter many facts throughout your daily life, but how many of them are relevant? The more focused energy you can invest in your vision by directing your thoughts with purpose, the higher probability of it materializing.

The only information that you should allow to consume you is relevant, factual information. If something is not helping you get to the next level or manifest your desires, there is no reason to invest excessive thought energy into it. Once you understand the power of focusing your thoughts, your life will change by coming into the present moment. Your life and thoughts must revolve around your vision if materialization is the goal. When you wake up, the first thing on your mind should be your desired destination, which will begin to show through internal habits.

As you direct more thought energy into your vision, time will make everything more clear. Implant a destination in your subconscious. Once a goal is accepted, your unconscious mind power comes to life. You will form new habits, ways of thinking, attract new information, and live new experiences.

When your mind focuses on irrelevant information, inner-power becomes diluted. Scattered thoughts are powerless. The mind can be detrimental or supernatural. If your energy is scattered, dispersed between multiple things, then overall power diminishes. Instead of wasting energy, invest your energy into fewer things. Focus on fewer things and observe the rate at which you grow.

The more energy you invest in growth, the sooner your desires will become a reality. The idea of chasing misleads many. The common thought is to pursue your dreams or chase success, but that is the opposite in real life. When you increase your value, the energy you produce will attract positive outcomes. The less energy wasted, the more energy that is reserved for things that enhance purpose. As a result, the ideas you receive will increase, and the number of material manifestations you experience.

Directed energy is the most powerful force on earth. What makes humans so powerful is their ability to control this force consciously. You can use your mind to generate power, just like a generator used for homes. Think of your mind as a continuous current of electricity. Once this mindset is adopted, a change initiates.

Many individuals waste energy throughout their day, investing in pointless activities and or purposeless thinking. When energy is reserved and controlled, it enhances overall power; power to create. There is a process called self-programming, which is widely used in the elite community. Imagine the mind as a computer.

All minds are programmed. Whether you understand the degree of this phenomenon, it is present and real. What separates the elite from the average is simple. Whoever understands the mind, combining science with the spiritual, develops supernatural like abilities. Once the formula is internalized, your concentrated intensity grows, which results in an ability to produce more energy.

In the beginning, it may be difficult to control your mind. The mind is a muscle. If you have not worked out in years, it will be impossible to go to the gym and lift the heaviest weights. Similarly, the mind that is not studied will have a difficult time maximizing the present moment. Another activity that increases thought power is visualization. To visualize requires you to enter the present and focus your mind on a specific idea for a particular amount of time.

Every morning, upon waking up, time should be set aside to imagine. The imagination faculty is real. Anything created in the imagination has the power of manifesting into reality. All great inventions began in the mind of someone. Visualization is not something that can be done once or twice. To become effective, it must become a habit. Positive habits grow into material gains acquired through productive action.

If you spend time visualizing every morning and night, your life will change. Your imagination allows you to create your future before it happens. The future is now. The future is in your present moment. When time is invested in imagining daily, experiences will transpire in a certain way. Some people feel like they have no control over their minds, but it is only due to a lack of action and

32

purpose. Your thoughts are a form of energy. Preserve and direct your energy with strategy.

Do not allow your thoughts to become scattered. Instead, dedicate more time to visualizing, praying, and meditating. In the beginning, it may be hard to sit and concentrate your thoughts for long periods, and there is a solution. Start with small time intervals. Focus on a specific goal for 20 minutes per day. Ten minutes in the morning and 10 minutes at night. Every day the goal should be to increase the amount of time set aside. Make out as many details as possible.

Self-programming is about rewiring the neural pathways in your brain. Whenever you think, act, see or imagine, neurons fire in your brain, creating neural pathways. The more you think with a definite purpose, visualize an image, or perform an action, the deeper the neural pathway becomes. Repeated activity plays a critical role in forming habits. Your neurons seek the easiest route or most traveled path because it requires the least amount of thought.

Humans are lazy creatures. You do not like to think, which is why you naturally form habits. You do not spend time thinking about walking, eating, talking, and many other automatic actions. Although brain activity is required, you don't feel, see, or think about it. Repetition has allowed these simple actions to sink below conscious thought while still being able to perform.

Imagine neural pathways as trails of snow. When it snows, a trail is left behind by whoever walked through the snow. For the second person, it is easier to follow the first and so on. By the end of the day, a path will be carved out, making it easier to walkthrough for the last person than the first person. Now translate that image to your mind.

Habits are practically automatic actions. When an action is repeated, it becomes easier for the body to create that action over time. Think about when you first learned to write. Much thought was required, making it hard for your hand to produce what your mind was seeing. Now when you write, it does not take thought at all.

The elite take advantage of this because they use it to learn new things and rapidly. Things become cemented in the mind because your neurons traveled that same path so many times. At a certain point, the route will become immortalized and automatic. Once you translate this science into a skill or field, your concentration will become immortalized within. The result will lead to new doors, naturally building generational wealth.

Habits are immortalized actions that make life easier. Instead of wasting conscious thought on lower-level aspects of the task, energy can be reserved for higher-level thinking and perceiving. Repetition creates habits and urges you to seek familiar patterns. The problem with this is that patterns can pose as illusions, which allows for manipulation and the creation of blind followers. Humans are very similar to computers and robots.

Your neural pathways begin with the thoughts you think and your environment. The key to recreating your reality is by rewiring neural pathways created by harmful environments, habits, and negative influences. Your mind does not know the difference between imagined experiences or real experiences; that is the true power of your mind. Take time to study mirror neurons. If you create the mental foundation of the life you desire, your outside reality will conform to the pathways created, through intuitive action, embedding essential habits.

Luck plays a large role in any endeavor. People often take luck for granted or completely dismiss the idea. Although that is a broad spectrum, there is a truth where a medium exists. The truth is that no man or woman can reach success without some form of luck. Luck is necessary, but it cannot be the only focus. Those who put in the work find luck more than those who do not make sacrifices. Over time your experiences will lead you to the destination that was created in mind.

The best way to use this information is by priming your mind for what is to come. Before deeper aspects are introduced, take a moment to analyze the act of writing. Writing is a significant step in success, yet many people ignore this powerful strategy. Writing for personal development is not promoted or taught in any school system or media outlet. Science backs the effects of writing.

Once understood, you can use this technique to program your mind. Research suggests that writing out concrete goals increases the odds of accomplishing them. Some studies show a pool of participants. One pool of participants writes out their goal. The other group does not write out a goal. The results displayed a higher goal completion rate amongst those who wrote down their goal.

Where do you deposit and withdraw money? The first thought that comes to mind is a bank. Now, imagine a vault, but instead of cash in the vault, replace it with your thoughts. Understand that thoughts are things. Humans cannot see thoughts, but they are more real than any physical entity. If you begin treating your thoughts like money, you will never think the same again.

Every moment you spend writing out your desires is an investment in the future. You can use a journal, the note section on your phone, or a computer to collect your thoughts. Writing is critical because it brings thoughts to life. The formless becomes visible, then transforms into something physical through repeated action. Have you ever wrote something down, then read it years later, to see that it has materialized? Just like you put money in a bank, you must store your thoughts somewhere.

When you put pen to paper, invisible thoughts are materializing into the physical reality. There are various phases to manifestation, and learning how to transform ideas into words, is one of the early stages. Many successful individuals keep journals. Journals allow you to store your thoughts somewhere. Words are powerful because they have a strong influence on your mind.

There must be precise detail to bring a vision to life. When your subconscious mind has an exact destination, it is easier to choose and attract a path leading you to your desires. No amount of luck can replace awareness from preparation. Every human on earth has a vision. What separates the successful people from the failures is the amount of energy invested in small details.

Write out the ideas you create in your mind. When words are written down, it crystallizes your vision. A force will begin to grow inside as your desires become more evident. Neurons fire in your mind whenever you spend time writing, thinking, or performing an action. Each task activates different parts of your brain. Brain activation allows you to internalize information or ideas in multiple ways.

The more ways you internalize something, the more a part of you it becomes. Research findings have suggested writing has many benefits. Studies have indicated that writing increases your memory, intelligence, and creativity, all topics discussed at different parts of this book. There is a power to writing things down. If you don't set time aside to write out your future, your future is controlled by everything and everyone but you.

Writing does not mean pages of information. When you write, be specific with your desires. How much money do you want to make? Who do you want to be? Where do you want to go? Do you want a job or a business? If you write down the answers to questions, you will attract events, people, and ideas leading you to destination in mind. Words crystalize what your mind visualizes.

The next step is action. Once the idea or vision is crystallized, there is nothing able to stop its materialization. Each experience in your life will direct you somewhere. Once your subconscious mind understands your desires, it will instinctually lead you to the obtainment of them. Writing needs to be a part of your process because it is integral to reprogramming and directing the human mind. Thoughts are things even though they cannot be seen, so it is also important to be definite in what you think and speak.

Words have power and enormous influence over your life's direction. Many people aren't conscious of the words they use, but depending on the words used, determines the outcome of a person's life. Words have been said to elicit frequencies and vibrations into the universe. Everything can be considered a form of energy.

When you speak, that energy or frequency is being broadcasted out into the universe. Energy attracts energy. In other words, what you speak will materialize into your life. Words will attract the material form into your life, so be wise with your words. The energy that you elicit is the energy that you receive.

Words create your reality. Without language or words, there would be no reality. Words allow humans to communicate and create mental images. If you see or hear the word money, you will produce a mental picture of money. If you hear or see love, you will create mental images of people you love or the things you love doing.

Once this clicks, you will have a greater command over life. When different affirmations and suggestions are learned, it is done through command. You must speak, think, write, and act out these affirmations. The more energy invested in your vision, the higher the odds become of manifesting your vision.

Many people speak of things that they do not want. They speak of things they hate. They speak of negative things, and as a result, they also attract negative things into their life. The energy created through speech and thoughts is also received back from the outside world. What is being created is a reciprocal effect. Once you become conscious, successful habits and beliefs will take over. The more you seek correct information, the more comfortable life will become.

This science is designed to help you control your mind and reality. The foundation starts with the thoughts that you implant within. One thing that you need to understand about information is that there is always more than one angle to look at something. You also need to know how to internalize the information and transform it into something that advances your mind, spirit, and life. With this information, you are given a template to program your mind for success. If you use the provided information, there will be an evident change in your life. These laws and practices are not new but old and able to relate to any period.

Part 3

Immortalize

The world that you live in requires the acquisition of skills. At the beginning of life, you could not walk, talk, think, read, or write. With time being the key ingredient, mere repetition has turned these, once foreign task, into an unconscious habit. You are now at a point where those tasks do not require thought, but it was not always that way.

Think back to the beginning stages of learning something new. When you engage in something new, your mind is fixated on the task. The amount of energy a beginner invests displays the real power of concentration, practice, and time. What happens as you begin to learn something?

The amount of concentrated focus required begins to fade. Why? Actions that initially needed conscious thought to become an innate habit. Once something becomes a habit, it can create complacency or ignite inspiration. Humans, by nature, like to take the easiest path. In other words, once a pattern is created, it is hard to reverse. Habits make life easy.

In contrast, inspiration can be ignited because of the power that can be gained. Once you learn how to create a habit around something, a new world will open for you. A world where you can analyze more profound concepts of a task. Legends, such as Kobe Bryant, display why programming habits have generational consequences when intense focus is sustained.

The human mind evolved to create habits because it allows you to use your conscious energy for other things. Another reason is that having to think requires energy, influencing you to develop and gravitate towards patterns. Could you imagine having to think while solving simple tasks? What if 100 percent concentration was needed to brush your teeth? Blow your nose? Drive your car?

In essence, habits make life simple or more difficult. What if you have bad habits? How can this manuscript benefit you if you have the right habits? The spiritual science of success begins and ends with the mind, deducing down to habits. Everything else is in between. Scientists have studied habits for centuries.

Expert researchers have examined these practices. Millionaires and billionaires, in all fields of life, have exercised these practices. What is the key to forming habits? Everything begins with understanding the present moment. That concept might sound basic, but take a moment to think. How much of your time is spent in the present?

What you may not realize is that little of your time is spent in the present moment. Take some time to think. How often do you think about the past? When is the last time you thought about your future? When your mind is focused on anything other than the present moment, you live in the past or future. It is impossible to go forward if you are always looking backward.

Present moment awareness takes some practice. You must focus energy on one task. When fully engaged, it is impossible to be aware of anything other than the experience itself. Life travels at a different frequency once you live in truth. Begin to analyze your mind's activity.

When does it drift away? Where does it wander? Self-analysis will not be easy, but you must take effect immediately. The act of practicing is a tool that you must learn to use efficiently and effectively. In this world, it is impossible to succeed without developing some set of skills.

As a human, you learn things without always having to be conscious of the process. The elite understands more profound components of the human mind than the average individual. When the mind is understood from a scientific point of view, it allows anyone to mentally, spiritually, and socially reach elite levels. From a fundamental perspective, the subconscious is that part of your mind that is not in focal awareness. What does this mean? Things are happening around you, but you are focused on one thing.

The subject of focus is your attention. Attention is your power because it is concentrated energy. Energy is the basis of all life-force, which was explained in part two. Without conscious energy, your environment is being scanned for danger, threats, your heart pumps, and your blood flows. The mind is always working, even without your effort. The subconscious is the part of your mind that is always on. Things make it into your subconscious, far beyond your awareness, which is why it is crucial to understand the difference between the unconscious.

The unconscious varies because it contains processes of the mind. What language do you speak? What motivates you? Who do you think about when you hear a love song? All of these things are unconscious actions that manifest through subconscious exposure. As your mind becomes more exposed to a specific subject, it will become permanent in your unconscious mind.

Action is the product of the unconscious, while embedding and absorption is the product of the subconscious. For example, Elite athletes take advantage

44

of this fact, manipulating the formula for their sport advancement. When playing a sport, most people are asleep while engaged, without even being aware. Sports are mainly instinct and reaction, two things that hardly require conscious thought. Once the athlete understands this, they can expose their subconscious mind to more in-depth aspects of their sport. The deliberate process of embedding leads to a definite outcome; unconscious actions elevating you to higher levels.

Athletes represent one group of people. Many successful individuals make use of these psychological practices. As a human, you are programmed for survival, which plays a large role in your operation. Imagine how difficult it would be if it required a conscious effort to make your heart pump. What if you had to activate the digestive system? The mind wants to make life easier, so most things become a product of the unconscious. The result creates room for the conscious mind to focus on higher aspects of the concentrated subject.

The conscious mind is the energy-producing mind. The less you have to focus on simple functions, the easier it is to operate through life. The same thing also applies to a field of study. Your source of power will increase once the conscious mind power is harnessed. The mind's ability to learn makes it possible for you to achieve anything with applied effort.

The subconscious mind contains all of your memories, experiences, thoughts, emotions, and ideas. The power of the subconscious mind: it does not know right from wrong. Whatever is introduced becomes truth. Truth creates beliefs, which influence actions and molds habits. What happens throughout life is that many people allow outside sources to form their beliefs, influencing their life's path.

From a young age, most humans begin to get programmed by the outside world. Once the early years of conditioning are complete, the young child enters into society, joining a school system, clubs, teams, and groups. Over time, the mind begins to conform to the environment. The environment will serve as food for the mind, which will significantly impact your reality and destination.

You may think you are making a decision in the present time, but the current is determined by what was allowed in the subconscious mind. The moment you take back control, a shift in your mind will ensue. There is much research suggesting the power of self-hypnosis, affirmations, auto-suggestions, and commands. What will elevate you is your ability to unlock different levels mentally.

The mental world creates the physical world. Nothing in the world you see is real. Everything in the material world was created in someone's mind. Many ignore the science of the mind, as well as the spirituality in nature. Awareness brings about completeness within.

All humans are connected to an infinite power source. Through present moment awareness, it is possible to connect to the endless power source. In the present moment, your energy is increased, laser focus is developed, and awareness is heightened. Once the present moment is mastered, your ability to learn new skills and improve the ones already equipped will rise exponentially. As a human being on this earth, you hold power not available to another species. With this power, you can take command of your reality, manifesting any desire growing within.

The power to influence your subconscious mind, then manifest into the physical world, is only available to humans. Some people live life unaware of the potential of knowing the relationship and functions of the brain and mind. You are consciously reading this passage, internalizing everything, but the deeper message is connecting with your subconscious. The elites have a different understanding of the mind. Their actions will suggest that a deep encoding of the universal laws was instilled at some point.

With life, nothing is for certain. You can plan. You can pray. You can believe, but all it takes is one experience. One experience is enough to change the direction of your life, either negatively or positively. With the universe, laws are certain.

There will always be a cause accompanied by an effect. In other words, once the laws are internalized, the result will always be a product of your choosing. Control in life comes once an individual knows how to program their mind. The conscious can influence and program the subconscious, which is the projector of your reality. Imagine yourself in a classroom with a teacher giving a lecture.

The teacher is using a projector that is connected to a computer. Now reorganize this image as the inner-mind. The first thing to connect is the projected result as reality. The screen represents the material world, while the projector represents your reality, and the computer your subconscious.

Whatever the projector is given, it will project, and that is what you will see. In life, your material world is influenced by your inner world. The teacher represents the conscious mind, while the computer represents the subconscious mind. Before class, the teacher is preparing what will be shown, using a computer to organize the data. This becomes practical once internalized because it can be used to learn anything.

The conscious mind, the teacher, chooses what goes into the subconscious mind, which creates the material, projected, world. When the present moment is sustained for countless hours, a skill, thought, or habit will be implanted in the subconscious, then materialize through the unconscious mind. When a skill is embedded within the subconscious mind, it becomes automatic, evolving into a habit and eventually crystallizing through the unconscious.

As you invest less conscious energy on low-level aspects, more focus can be reserved for the higher functioning tasks. This will transform into more extraordinary skills, heightened awareness, and longer times spent in the present moment. It is sometimes mistaken, causing individuals to believe the conscious, attention focused mind is the ruler, but it is not.

A key to reaching excellence is by embedding a particular skill or set of skills within your subconscious so that it becomes a part of your nervous system. Once that truth is accepted, a more in-depth analysis activates. There are so many talented, skilled, and gifted individuals, but what becomes the separating factor? Expectations can be tied to products or a result. For instance, two people may be talented musically but end up on two different journeys.

Sometimes it will seem as though one person is further ahead because of talent. Often people can be driven by the product, not the process. When a person has material expectations, what can happen is a false sense of security. For moments the material manifestations will seem to fill a void. Once the excitement wears off, the desire for more, naturally, takes control.

The reality of something, once experiencing it, can be the opposite of initial belief. This may be due to the optimism individuals initially possess towards things they don't have but want. Once a millionaire becomes a millionaire, by nature, their desire for more will increase.

Why live in the same area? Why drive the same car? These are not problems. As you make more, it is normal to spend more. The despair comes when material goals are the only focus. Those who leave behind legacies and build generational wealth are obsessed with the process, not the product. This is how two people can be on the same path but reach different destinations. The internal desire plays a large role in the levels that you make it to.

Do not become confused. Material things are healthy. There is nothing wrong with wanting abundance. Never allow anyone to plant that idea in your mind. Although the material cannot be the only driving force. In other words, there must be some genuine emotions derived from a higher source that generate purpose.

Humans are spiritual beings. Your mind is invisible. Your thoughts are invisible, but the invisible influences the physical. When you learn how to maintain present-moment focus, it will become apparent that any material item can be thought into existence. No gain will ever be enough if that is all that motivates you.

Those who fall in love with the process love the idea of perfection, knowing it is only something to aim for but not obtain. What is perfection? There is a textbook definition: the condition, state, or quality of being free from all flaws. Then there is a real-world definition. The direction in which elites aim, with a conscious understanding of growth, through repetition.

True perfection is not finite; it is not tangible. Perfection is nothing more than an idea, based on your present moment, along with perspective. From person to person, the concept will vary. In other words, it is not real. Your view of what is perfect is only based upon where you are currently. It will always move away from you.

Observe where your attention is focused daily. Are you in the past, future, or present? Once you learn to enter the present moment, through repetition and eventually making it a habit, one thing will become apparent to you. In the present moment, you are in a perfect state of mind due to the unison formed with the universal consciousness. To enter the present moment is to suppress all emotions and succumbed to laser focus.

Your ego creates false ideas of perfection. As you evolve, what you envision as perfect will shift with your present circumstances and perspective. Nature doesn't have an ego, so do not allow yours to take control of you. The less self-aware you are, the easier it will be for your ego to get in the way. The ego can be referred to as the decision-making component of your personality.

The ego purpose is to work by reason, along with society's norms and rules. From a grounded perspective, people who are not self-aware struggle with the ego because they do not perceive society or themselves. They allow their desires and beliefs to influence adverse decisions based on bad judgment. Furthermore, it is easy to understand why perfection is only an idea.

The secret to achieving true perfection is by coming into the present moment. The present state of mind allows for universal consciousness to be accessed. The conscious being in you, the mind that thinks, has a strong, unstoppable force when infused with directed purpose.

One of your most significant abilities is to self-analyze. The more you learn about yourself, the higher you will be able to rise. Beyond that, to know thyself is to know everyone else.

From a scientific perspective, humans are naturally the same. Basic functioning and desires are consistent throughout the average person. What can be done with this information? When people have greater expectations for something, what can happen is sadness. If there is an idea that things should be a certain way, it can cause despair. To love the process is to accept where one is at that moment in time, with a drive to improve.

Aiming for perfection is encouraged because it encourages you to grow and elevate. The danger comes if you become fixated with perfection. Take a more in-depth look at this in the world of basketball. Look at the route of two basketball players. Both individuals are great shooters. They can make difficult jump shots from all areas of the court.

At one point, they are very close in overall skill level. Five years pass, and there becomes a clear distinction in ability. Both go on to play division one basketball, but one goes pro, and the other does not. What takes place? The transition happens because of the love one had for the process and the other for the product.

Any master of a field will tell you there is no such thing as knowing enough. If the time is invested, there is no limit to how great you can be. With purpose, directed purpose, many energies will enter your life, desirable and undesirable. When you become driven because of the optics, or the benefits, there is a loss of control. Focusing on the process allows you to remove emotions from the equation.

How is that possible? If purpose is the focus, then something is understood. The moment in which you are is the situation you are supposed to be in. In other words, there is magic in the present moment. Think back to the day you learned how to drive a car. How difficult was it for you at first?

How easy is it for you now? There is one significant difference that you will immediately notice. The amount of time you spent thinking, when learning, versus the amount of time you spend thinking now, is vastly different. How does that relate? As a beginner, your mind is not aware of the information it is receiving. Instead of being able to "multi-task,"; performing multiple actions at once, more attention must be placed on the task at hand.

Over time, your mind forms a habit of the process through laser focus, and less conscious thought is required to perform the action. This information becomes powerful once you learn how to use it to your advantage. The elite are highly skilled people who are more adept at specific fields than most of the population. Some people may be unconsciously aware of these practices and laws but still, implement them. The real power is when you bring it to your consciousness, increasing overall precision.

To become elite at something, hours must be invested. Striving with purpose replaces acting on emotion with self-awareness and patience. When you become an observer of self, you are placed in the driver seat. All humans feel emotions, which are engines to act. There is energy attached to all emotions, which is why you must know how to retain it.

Growth is aiming for perfection, knowing that it is not possible to obtain. Although perfection is merely an idea, aiming for it t provides direction. As you observe yourself in the process, begin to learn behaviors and habits. Do not allow habits to grow from emotions such as greed, envy, or uncertainty. Think about that. Each emotion that you feel creates a desire to act.

Habits form through repeated actions. In other words, the more energy you focus, with a definite purpose, your emotions will guide you by creating habits within. To become elite, you must invest more hours. You must understand that repetition will not be fun, but it comes with great benefits. To bring your mind to the present moment, focusing all your energy on one task is powerful.

Humans are creatures of habit. Turn your passions into habits. What you practice will become a habit. Knowing this can work in your favor. Habits are natural actions that internalize within. They are done intuitively, without thought.

Responses happen because they are a natural part of your behavior. Make self-awareness and reflection more natural. Bring your goals to your awareness daily. Work on your vision every day. There is a power to feeling as if you possess something.

The emotions you feel influence you intuitively. When you learn where you want to go precisely, then it is time to study the path. The better you understand the motions you must intentionally repeat, to accomplish the goal, an admiration will develop for the process. You cannot change what you are unaware of. There are some people with talent or potential but are not aware of how to mentally reach the elite level.

The mental is what separates good, great, and elite. Once you bring something to your conscious awareness, it is impossible to unsee. Once you learn precisely how to manipulate the habits you develop and emotions you feel through concentrated thought, a new world will open up for you. It is a fact that the mind is a complex entity, but many things have been identified through the ages. One thing, in particular, is the two minds that exist within.

There is a conscious, attention focusing mind. In contrast, it has been suggested there is also a subconscious, automatic instinctual mind at the forefront of survival. Your conscious mind can create a type of energy, which increases your ability to focus and embed commands and desires. On the flip side, the subconscious mind is much more instinctual, playing a large role in your survival. There can be a misunderstanding of the subconscious mind power because it does not require actual thought. Your conscious thoughts influence your subconscious to respond and react in future events.

Not only does your conscious mind program your subconscious, but your surroundings as well. Far beyond your awareness, the subconscious mind is working, scanning the environment, pumping your heart, and creating your reality. The common mistake is the trust that is put into the conscious mind. Consciousness does not play the role that some people often believe. The barrier between greatness and average is all in the mind. Great individuals understand a different mind state is required throughout their journey.

If greatness is desired, you must learn how to use your conscious mind to program your subconscious mind and influence positive unconscious action. Self-programming is about taking control and recreating your reality. Over time you will create experiences that put you in a position to manifest your desires. The result of these experiences will be a physical representation of the suggestions that were affirmed. If time is not invested in mental development, growth will taper off.

It is easy to allow the outside world to consume you, ignoring the importance of directed thought. What will take place is the scattering of thought, which will lead to a stream of bad events—negative influences, subconsciously, program you to feel or act in destructive ways. The best way to program your mind is by using something called auto-suggestion. Auto-suggestion has been studied by researchers for centuries.

Suggestions program your subconscious mind through powerful phrases and beliefs. Many researchers believe that auto-suggestion is the most powerful way to influence your subconscious mind. Your subconscious mind is what creates your reality. If auto-suggestion is used to control your subconscious mind, you alter your future reality by using directed thought. Suggestions are phrases or beliefs, stated in the third or second-person perspective, about yourself. In other words, you are speaking about yourself, as if you are not yourself.

Suggestions remove the internal perspective and place you outside of yourself. The outside perspective allows you to tap into an external power source, better known as universal consciousness. Words such as he, she, you, or your name gives you a completely different perception of yourself. This will have a psychological and spiritual effect on the mind if the process is repeated over time. Suggestions draw out higher powers, which increases the chances of you achieving success.

Auto-suggestion reveals itself through the name. For these phrases or suggestions to work, it must become automatic. In other words, these phrases and suggestions must be repeated or always thought of daily. The repetition process will embed these beliefs into your subconscious and become a part of you, making the phrases automatic. You must set time aside to do this every day.

Auto-suggestions help you direct your mind to the correct destination. What are your dreams? Do you want to impact the world? When do you want it to happen? Those questions can be answered and instilled through suggestions. Questions force you to look at your life from an aerial view.

Speaking to yourself from different perspectives also enhances your view of life. Perspective is everything, and the greater your perception becomes, the easier it will be to navigate through life. When your subconscious creates your reality, it will be based on the implanted suggestions and affirmations. Once you learn how to embed them, life will travel in any direction that you desire.

Experiences materialize based on the suggestions embedded in your subconscious mind. The basis of immortalizing a skill starts with understanding the relationship between habits and subconscious exposure. It does not matter what skill or field is chosen. Science will provide the same result; more subconscious exposure results in unconscious action. This phenomenon allows your conscious mind to focus on higher aspects of the task, creating opportunities for advancement.

The elite take advantage of this psychological law by mastering a skill and using it to create opportunities. Begin with what you are natural at. Once it is found, implant more unconscious actions through subconscious exposure. As your understanding grows for the concentration, the skill will become immortalized within, given you supernatural like abilities. There is a lot of information in this world, but how much of it is factual?

Beyond the facts, how much of it can benefit you? If you are taking in the wrong information, it will be easy for your mind to create situations that don't reflect the desires that you have within. Many people ignore the research part because it is not the most fun. Research means reading, experimenting, and reaching out to individuals for information, connections, and support. When you do not have the history or credibility, people are less likely to invest in you, believe in you, or want to do business with you. The beginning challenges you mentally, but life will direct you to the right places as long as you seek and act.

Research provides information to acquire your desires. The vision that you create needs the information to come to life. Once you internalize the correct information, it will be easier to use auto-suggestions and affirmations. If you feed your mind bad information, you will go in the opposite direction of your desired destination. Refer back to the car analogy.

If you put the wrong fuel in a car, then it will not go anywhere. If you are filling that same car with the correct fuel, then the vehicle will travel. The human mind is very impressionable. Conduct research because if you never take a look outside of your perspective, it will be hard to rise to the highest of the highs.

The higher up you go in life, the more aware you have to be. If you are stuck in your environment and only consume the information you are given, you may almost always be misled. Sometimes you may have to go outside of your immediate environment and search for new information.

Once you begin to search for information, apply the information to create experiences in real-life situations. Applied knowledge equals wisdom. Wisdom is powerful because it can not only be used, but it can also be given back. The information you are feeding your mind will determine what direction you go in and if you can get there.

Make sure you take advantage of all the resources around you. That will continuously keep your mind open. If you are digesting the correct information, applying it, using suggestions and affirmations, you will consistently experience things that put you in a position to win.

Part 4

<u>Install</u>

Encoding intelligence means knowing how to interpret the data that your mind receives from its environment and the society that it is involved with. Everything that enters your mind can be considered data. Information is received in your mind as data, then outputs a physical image in the form of an experience. Your outside world is a direct reflection of the data which your mind consumes.

It is crucial to control the data that enters your mind. Affirming is one of the most common tools used to bring suggestions to life. Once neural pathways are created through visualization, which affirmations are a product of, intuitive, unconscious actions will crystallize habits.

Elite people use the tandem of affirmations and suggestions to reach a higher level in their chosen field. Affirming beliefs act as a crystallization process because it makes you, the subject, command your envisioned destination's emotion and energy. What transpires after is a development of habits, which action is derived. Visualization creates an internal firing and wiring of neurons in your brain. The process of visualization is identical to performing an action.

When you envision something, it creates a neural pathway for later actions to develop. Once you learn what actions are needed to put you closer to the goal you previously visualized in your mind, you can become more precise. Precision decreases the likelihood of error. You must be explicitly encoding things into your brain that heighten intelligence.

Intelligence is the ability or awareness to know how to consume and use information. How a person feels about the destination affects their energy. Whoever feels more connected, emotionally or spiritually will reach the destination before someone who does not have that internal desire.

When a belief or idea is affirmed, the energy within begins to interact with the energy on the outside. The result is experience, material manifestations, new opportunities, and visible signs. Nature is nothing but a subset born from the original, universal laws. Affirmations allow a person to manipulate their mind because once a person commands their greatness, genius, and higher power, an equal source of energy comes to life.

What takes place is the birth of new experiences. Wisdom becomes the product of all experiences, which is nothing more than applied knowledge. In other words, a person not only has the idea of what the information will create but an actual product, in an experience, of what the information produces. Instead of an idea of what will happen, wisdom is the enlightenment of nature combined with spirituality.

Science allows you to master something. Once you remove the error from an equation, you can achieve success at a higher level and faster. This is what the elite do. These psychological laws are enough to manipulate the understanding and awareness of all humans. The individual who interprets this data, programming success, will receive a heightened intelligence.

In short, you are being placed in the driver's seat of your life. This is the driver seat of your actions and mind. What you are being allowed to do is see more significant aspects of the skills you have equipped, allowing for more opportunities. If you want to understand a field or skill on an elite level, it begins with how you manipulate your mind's inner workings.

Without understanding how to program the mind, it will be impossible to fully control your life. The outside world begins with your inner, mental world. What do you spend most of your time thinking about? How has your environment played a role in programming you? The true power inside can be harnessed, by understanding the relationship, between the conscious, subconscious, and unconscious.

Words are a misunderstood concept because their power goes undetected. Many people know the saying "watch what you speak," but it could not be more accurate. Words are the building blocks of society and human communication. What happens when you hear or read the word cow? The unconscious reaction creates an image inside of your mind.

Humans can create images in their minds. This is a power that is only available to humans. The imagination faculty is the warehouse that produces your dream life. Action is what transforms that data into an experience. Words are important to understand because it is the basis of encoding your mind.

When words are spoken, mental images are created, causing neurons to fire in the brain. Being able to live the life you envision begins with how aware you are. Words form the base that your dream develops its structure. The amount of effort you invest in your vision's details determines the outcome of your path. As you become more specific, using exact dates, goals, and destinations, a transformation will occur.

What happens as you begin to incorporate detail? There is something known as affirmations. These are phrases about yourself that accept beliefs or challenge negative thoughts and patterns. Research has suggested that affirmations are an extremely effective way to influence the subconscious mind. Many people have heard of the concept, for it has been discussed and studied for centuries, but sadly only a few capitalize from the latent power.

The most powerful phrase in the English language is "I am." Phrases can be used as affirmations or suggestions. The textbook definition for suggestion is something that implies a certain fact. On the contrary, to affirm means to declare as a fact.

The combination of both methods gives you access to multiple sources of power. Auto-suggestion implies, meaning that the source of power comes from the outside. Something is implied about one's self. Affirmations declare, meaning, the power comes from within. When these concepts are used in unison, the unconscious mind will lead you to the final destination of whatever you implant.

Beliefs must be affirmed in various ways. You can use speech, meaning you speak aloud, a phrase, multiple times throughout the day. Another effective way is through directed thought, thinking of some destination, goal, or idea, with intense focus. Writing specific phrases is also another effective way to program the mind.

Once the belief is affirmed through continuous sight, hearing, speech, or writing, it takes life in the subconscious mind. Science has shown that repetition is an efficient way to influence the mind. These practices and laws cannot only be done once or for a few years. This must become a way of life, with no emotional attachment to time, in relation to location.

The journey of mental development will require some time because of the reconditioning and conditioning process that must occur. If your mind affirms a belief, actions will take life with little thought. Specific actions will become habits, which will confirm the beliefs that are inside of you. In other words, the beliefs that you currently hold play a large role in the current position you are in.

Everything around you is received and broadcasted by your subconscious mind. The subconscious is the creator and projector of your material world. Beyond that fact, the subconscious is heavily influenced by the ideas you speak, think, or write. A sad truth is that sometimes negative beliefs are adopted from outside sources. Many times the result can lead to lifelong trauma.

If negative beliefs were instilled, then a person will act in destructive ways due to their environment's invisible programming. If you are not in control of your thoughts, then you are not in control of yourself. Encoding the mind is simple but requires effort, repetition, and patience. Auto-suggestion becomes more potent once you incorporate affirmations as well. One should not be used without the other.

Language is the foundation of social life. There is a science to how words can be impressed upon the mind. These two concepts can be viewed as tools. Tools are powerless when misused, yet powerful when used effectively. You are being presented with a tool that will only exhibit power if used effectively, repeatedly, and consciously.

The correct use of affirmations places you in the driver seat. The main key to understanding this concept is knowing that you speak to yourself from a first-person perspective. The phrase I am, I have, and I can, attached to a belief, forms a connection to a later experience that crystallizes what is believed.

The result of planting affirmations will begin to materialize through repeated habits. What gives you power is your ability to program through repetition. Once you start incorporating this concept, you will use phrases that create the life that you desire. When beliefs are affirmed, a transformation occurs internally. Habits are created based on what a person believes about themselves or reality in general.

For example, a person who does not believe they can make more than $5,000 per month will rarely experience making $5,000 per day. The power of mental encoding is potent. A person who lacks confidence can utilize this information to implant confidence within. What literally happens is an altering of perception through mind manipulation.

What can truly be defined as real? In other words, beliefs ground the foundation that the structure is built on. New seeds, also thoughts, must be planted, and old roots must be cured or removed. If a specific phrase is repeated enough times, your subconscious mind will accept the idea as true. The belief will come alive through intuitive and unconscious actions, which later form into habits. You may not realize that some of your negative habits were built on beliefs that were not implanted consciously.

The standards that you set reveals numerous things about your beliefs. Beliefs reveal who a person is at the core. Once this is understood, it becomes apparent why emotions are so connected to overall thought power. One of the most important emotions to know how to produce is confidence. Those who are confident are certain about their beliefs, with no acknowledgment of doubt.

Greatness is a belief and closely tied to the emotion of confidence. When you affirm your greatness, emotions such as confidence, excitement, and love will exude you. Emotions influence actions; thoughts and beliefs influence emotions, and actions create habits. In other words, be deliberate and intentional about what you do, say, and think.

It can be easy to fall out of love, quit the process, or turn around, but that is the quickest way to meet failure. Fear is an emotion; failure is a belief. The only way you can fail is by believing you have failed. Those who encounter continuous failure do so because of their self-image. When you do not see yourself as good enough, your mind will attract those beliefs' material manifestations.

The idea of failure produces fear that comes alive in all areas of life. Confidence is a necessary trait to adopt when striving for success. The more time you take to affirm your own beliefs, the more confident you will be throughout your journey. If you are not confident during the process, it will be easy to stop or quit. There will be a lot of things that make you want to stop. Only a percentage of people will support or believe in the beginning, which makes taking risk difficult.

Whatever exists outside of your awareness has no possibility of control or understanding. Without power, achieving your dreams will be unlikely. Be aware of each thought that you think because it has a more significant impact on your future. Do not fall into the trap of desiring the product more than the process. Satisfaction is short-lived, with material gains.

When you fall in love with the process, you understand that it will involve years of programming your mind with your own beliefs and ideas. Nothing truly exists outside of your present moment. In other words, never get caught up in what is out of your control. The idea of a dream is not tangible. Dreams are meant to provide directional guidance. Create the destination to get the direction, but the final result will always be more satisfying than your initial perception.

Think about the beginning stages of life. Babies learn about the world through observation and mere exposure. When exposed to something, for long enough, with or without your awareness, it will become engrained in your mind. The relevance is beliefs. Many people develop their beliefs from their surroundings.

Your self-image, idea of love, and understanding of emotions were mostly learned through exposure, not conscious awareness. The longer you do something, not only will it become easier, but more unconscious, giving your conscious mind more freedom to focus. Humans can learn without practicing or even thinking. Practice encompasses learning, but not vice versa. The advantage goes to you when beliefs and desires are affirmed consciously, through repetition and practice.

How do you create the direction? What does the direction do for you? The concept of affirmations is vital to practice because it gives you the ability to create direction. Instead of allowing the past or early conditioning to dictate your destination and reality, enter the driver seat by becoming conscious and aware. The moment you take control of your thoughts, your future will be forever changed.

Many scientists have spent years studying affirmations. Studies have explained the positive, psychological effects in a variety of ways. Affirmations help you direct your thoughts by implanting specific beliefs, ideas, and habits, into the subconscious mind. Affirmations are the power within because thoughts are definite and directed. Any phrase that is repeated enough becomes one with your mind, body, and soul.

An individual who looks in the mirror every day and says, "I am beautiful," radiates with a certain energy and begins to embody that truth. Confidence will start to grow within, and that confidence will be displayed, through unconscious reactions, to the outside world. Now, take that same example, and apply it to someone who tells themselves the complete opposite.

Beauty is in the eye of the beholder. A person who sees themselves as ugly communicates that through habits formed by beliefs. When a belief such as not good enough comes to life, it shows through quitting, pessimistic thoughts, and destructive behaviors. Actions are influenced through beliefs, and beliefs are learned.

Affirmations direct the power and the energy within. The gut feelings, also known as intuition, that arise are direct signs. Intuitive action creates experiences through the law of attraction, which transcends to manifestation. Your mental energy can be enhanced and directed through these practices. Once energy is created, the next step is direction.

Intuitive action means to create experiences through the inner desires that you have, even if you are not sure of the outcome. Many people refer to this as a risk, but with no risk, there are no rewards. When you begin acting out of intuition, you will attract money, people, experiences, and ideas into your life. That is why affirmations are so powerful. You are conditioning your mind for future experiences through words and thoughts that you have not lived.

Imagine your mind as a vehicle. Your consciousness is the driver. The conscious mind is responsible for directing the subconscious mind, referred to as the vehicle. If you do not direct your subconscious, then it will be easy to end up lost, in a place, not knowing where you made a mistake. If you get in a car but do not have a precise destination or the directions to get to your final destination, you will end up lost. The same thing happens in life.

Affirmations give you a target and route. Daily, you must implant beliefs and desires through powerful phrases. Your subconscious mind must know what you want. When you implement action, or when the car begins driving, it does not matter which route you take. There will be mistakes along the way, but the final destination will be great.

Experiences are life's greatest teacher. In other words, without taking risks, growth will never occur. All information is not useful. The misconception that many have is that beliefs are always true. Just because you are born into something does not mean it is true or right.

You must conduct your own research. There is a lot of information in this world, but how much of it is factual?

Beyond the facts, how much of it can benefit you? If you are taking in the wrong information, it will be easy for your mind to create situations that do not reflect the desires within. Many people ignore the research aspect because it is not the most fun.

Research means reading, experimenting, and asking questions. These steps are hard for some individuals. You must know how to ask the right questions. You must know how to find the correct books. In this phase, you may have to reach out to many individuals for information, connections, and support. Research can be challenging because people are less likely to invest in you, believe in you, or do business with you when you do not have the history or credibility.

The beginning challenges you mentally, but as long as you seek and act based on intuition, life will direct you to the right places. Research provides information to acquire your internal desires. The vision that you create needs information to come to life. Once you internalize the correct information, it will be easier to use auto-suggestions and affirmations. If you feed your mind bad information, you will go in the opposite direction of your desired destination.

If you put the wrong fuel in a car, then it will not go anywhere. If you are filling that same car with the correct fuel, the vehicle will travel. The human mind is very impressionable. Conducting research is important because it forces you to enhance your perspective. The greater your perspective becomes, the easier it will be to rise to the highest level.

The higher up you go in life, the more aware you have to be. Sometimes you may have to go outside of your immediate environment and search for new information. An aerial view of society is crucial because it allows you to study people. Although people are very different, the mind works the same from person to person.

The better you understand other people, the better you will understand yourself, vice versa. Once this happens, society, and the people in it, will register in your mind differently. Slowly, you will begin studying people, learning their habits, and triggers. Once you understand how to write your own reality and create your own future, the direction to take will become clearer.

After searching for information, apply the information to create experiences in real-life situations. Applied knowledge equals wisdom. Wisdom is power, and power is nothing more than controlling and directing energy. The information you are feeding your mind will determine what direction you go in and if you can get there.

Self-development is essential. Take advantage of all the resources around you. That will require you to keep your mind open. If you are digesting the correct information, applying it, using suggestions and affirmations, you will consistently experience things that put you in a position to win.

The way to change old beliefs is through a step by step process. The first step involves questioning. Once a belief comes into question, it will drive you into discover mode. The object is to find evidence that proves or disproves. Once the final verdict is made, the subconscious mind will begin to create a matching reality.

Intelligence and beliefs are closely linked to success. The interplay of both auto-suggestion and affirmations gives you an ability to manipulate your mind and future. It can be confusing to understand, but conscious awareness will connect data to experiences in the outside world. Then it will take creativity to put all of the pieces together.

Part 5

Creative Genius

The acquisition of wisdom takes creativity. Many people living in society are afraid to be creative. People wake up every day hiding from the truth. To be clear, creation is a high form of intelligence; it goes beyond knowledge recall, extending into knowledge creation.

Intellect is knowledge learned. Wisdom is knowledge experienced. Those who rise to the highest levels know how to yield wisdom from information application. Information is available to each human being, especially with the internet. Two people who internalize the same information will produce two distinct life experiences due to a difference in application.

The mind is nothing more than the brain in action. When information is produced into a physical experience, something invisible has become visible. Once you learn how to yield the maximum amount from experiences, intuition will help guide you. Mere consumption will not lead to results; you must effectively use the information you consume.

To be creative requires the embracing of novelty. Intuition, on the other hand, arises in the form of an inner, gut feeling. The projection of unknown possibilities leads to an urge to act. It is not enough to be knowledgeable. Once the spiritual nature within is combined with information for knowledge creation, a superior power will be unlocked.

An intelligent person can be knowledgeable, but that does not mean they are creative. Creativity requires a novel form of intelligence that is of a higher order. Many people do not know that creativity is the key that unlocks and gives you access to infinite intelligence. What is infinite intelligence? Infinite intelligence can be explained as the limitlessness of endlessness in space, impossible to measure or calculate. To possess this type of mind, power places you in a position to rise to extreme heights.

The difference between intelligence and creativity is that one embraces retaining and recalling mass amounts of information—the other embraces individuality and knowledge creation. To create something means that it began as data in the mind and materialized into something that can be seen with the eyes. The combination of creativity and intelligence makes it so that nothing is a limitation in this universe but the universe itself.

Creativity is essential when combined with the desire to manifest a goal. The sad truth is that there are History classes, but not Future classes. There are Geometry classes, but not Money Management or Investment classes. The American school system does not promote creativity or teach you how to be more creative, which is a problem.

In school, you are taught to conform and follow the rules. The effect of groupthink is suppression. Those who go outside the norm get chastised, and those who follow are praised. That is why there is a lack of creativity in society as a whole. A change will never come until the truth is brought to the consciousness of individuals.

Creativity is closely connected to the spiritual. What is the spiritual? Your invisible world can be considered spiritual. The belief in a God or higher power is spiritual. There is no physical evidence of its existence in this world, but belief alone makes it present in your reality. There is no right or wrong. The person that does not believe will just not have the ability to see.

A question that someone could pose is the existence of thoughts. You are not able to see thoughts, but you can think, correct? Or is it all in your mind? To live in this world means doing so blindly. That is why faith, unwavering faith, is so important to have.

When the mind believes something exists, it automatically takes life in reality, which can be dangerous or rewarding. There is no physical evidence of the invisible existence. The spiritual only exists in your mind. As long as you have faith in your beliefs, then your beliefs will become true. When creativity is adopted, then used to produce wisdom, a newfound control comes to life.

Creativity is a skill, and being creative comes when you are free, mentally free. When you are free, the mind is not controlled by anyone but you. To be free means converting ideas into experiences that lead to overall advancement. With practice and awareness, it is possible to enhance these abilities for higher rates of success.

Information enters the mind as invisible data. Applied information exits the mind as a concept. What is retrieved from that concept can be added to the internal data to be transformed into wisdom. The acquisition of wisdom enhances your overall power source. Wisdom gives you answers to unsolved equations. The information inside of you is not complete without the other variable, also known as real life.

The ability for experiences to be extracted from the mind, for conscious analysis, as a physical experience, proves that you a creator. Close observation of outcomes gives you the ability to manipulate variables for desired results. Once you know what an action creates in the outside world, then with science, you know how to produce the same result. When you learn this science, you begin to creatively encode experiences that bring ideas and wisdom to life.

Creativity is the ability to do something naturally in a distinctive way. Every individual on this Earth has some type of uniqueness about themselves. The difficulty for some is learning how to express it. To encode intelligence goes far beyond what you can see because it's an internal process that affects you lifelong.

Creativity lives in the mind, so does thoughts and information. Once you understand how to effectively use information to create valuable experiences, an unconscious state will take over in important times. Sometimes the state is referred to as flow. The only thing that the subconscious mind needs is exposure. It absorbs and detects everything.

The more you expose yourself to something, the chances are higher that it will become embedded into your subconscious mind. The goal should be to implant your desires, crafts, and beliefs into your subconscious mind. Once the subconscious mind has been influenced, nature will do the rest.

That is the power of the subconscious mind. That is the secret to becoming naturally gifted. Find your passion and implant it in your subconscious mind with creative techniques that are natural for you. The only way to take control of your life is to take control of your subconscious mind. Manipulate what you are exposed to by surrounding yourself with a specific stimulus.

You will notice an intuitive feeling taking over that causes action. That is the creative energy that is coming from the universe. Life seems to travel a certain way during this time, as more ideas spring from your subconscious. The subconscious activates the unconscious, and that is what the elites rely on to excel. Unconscious states allow your mind to do most of the task, while your conscious energy focuses on higher aspects.

When endeavoring to understand a new task, your mind becomes completely absorbed. You suddenly sink into a new state of mind, producing new ideas with an intense focus. Time is an essential ingredient, if not the most important, through this entire process. Time is vital due to the power of consistent practice. The whole process, from beginning to end, rewires your mind, enhancing creativity.

Slowly but surely, elements of any concentration or skill become hardwired. In other words, you internalize the craft, making it apart of your nervous system. With countless hours of practice and exposure, your mind begins to discover new approaches through creative methods. With new techniques, new experiences are born, meaning an increase in wisdom.

When you are awakened to the hidden abilities, a miraculous connection is made. What makes spiritual science so powerful is that it doesn't require any initial skill. Dedication is needed, which is committing, through any condition, no matter your circumstance. Those who do learn, with a pre-learned skill, take their talent to an elite level. Along the way, many obstacles will appear, but that is normal.

Every master, all of the greats, the gifted, the genius, experienced setbacks, especially in the beginning. Repeated exposure is the secret to enhancing the mental foundation for mind power. The result will be growth while negative emotions fade. When you learn how to creatively expose yourself to a specific concentration, the less your mind will concentrate on low-level aspects, and skill level will be heightened.

Part 6

Supreme Control

When you master the science of mind, a new world will become available. In part six, memory, emotion, concentration, and habits will be detailed further. These components of the mind are essential to understand because it completes the equation. Once it is clear how these processes work, there will be more control of your actions' results.

The mind is a machine. When one function is improved, it can change the functioning of the entire entity. When you control what happens within, the power of encoding will be revealed. Beyond encoding, it will become clear how concentration, along with memory and emotion, can be used to advance mentally. Once the memory faculty is deduced down to a basic formula, the way in which habits are created will be fully realized.

When you learn what works and what does not, it can increase the amount of time you spend doing things that work. Science allows you to become a master of something through the use of formulas. There are mental formulas, formulas that have been shared, allowing you to change your brain's wiring. The foundation of your brain and life begin and end with memory.

The world that you see, with your eyes, is not what is collected by the mind. The outside world enters your mind as data. The data is then encoded into the brain, where patterns originate from. Most of what you do on a daily basis, or see, registers in your mind as a pattern. What does this mean? The brain works by following and recognizing patterns, which is a critical ingredient in forming a habit.

Memories play a large role in wiring the brain. If the brain works by detecting patterns, then manipulating memories would mean altering future events. Identities are formed by memories created from past experiences. The most powerful memories are those which have emotion attached. Emotions have a way of engraining experiences in your memory deeper.

The identity you form is controlled by the ego. As mentioned in part three, the ego can be referred to as your personality's decision-making component. The purpose of the ego is to work by reason, along with society's norms and rules. People who are not self-aware struggle with the ego because they do not perceive society or self from a grounded perspective. Once you understand how to control your emotions and your reactions, a transition will happen.

As you can see, everything in your mind is, in some way, connected. To change one component means another function will be affected. To understand the mind, learning the interconnectedness of these functions will play a large role. Emotions release chemicals in the brain when the mind is exposed to a trigger. Emotions arise in the mind but transport through the entire body, creating feelings, influencing actions and moods.

Emotions cannot be seen with the physical eye. Many do not know what is happening behind the scenes of their mind. Your memory's foundation was built on the most powerful experiences, which have influenced your habits and destination. The habits you possess form your identity, and your identity creates the material world around you. What you identify with controls the outside world around you. Powerful experiences stay with you until death, such as trauma.

Why do you think trauma creates so many wounds? The emotion combined with the real-world experience primes the mind for later retrieval. Memories with emotionally charged energy can have dangerous or rewarding outcomes. Traumatic experiences cause some individuals to repeatedly make destructive choices throughout life. Some examples are committing crimes, acts of violence, or extreme detachment. Knowing the effects of emotion and memory can help you change your identity.

Victims of trauma do not understand the biochemical reactions of reliving an experience. When a traumatic event is relived, anger, pain, sadness, and fear activate inside the body. What then transpires is an embodiment of these feelings, which transform into material equals. When you feel pain, more attention is placed on pain, which deepens the wound. From this perspective, a stream of destructive events can manifest. From an elite perspective, an equally positive result will come to life.

When you learn how to use your imagination faculty, you learn how to engineer chemical reactions. The act of visualizing creates neural pathways for future decision making. When it is time to decide, intuition will guide you, which is an instinctual feeling within. Intuition works because the neural system was primed for that moment through the precise use of the imagination.

Intuition leads to action because the feeling arises for an act to be committed. The experiences you create from acts influenced by intuition form long term memories. These memories will be positively charged with emotion and yield much wisdom. Memories are created by interacting with the outside world through the five senses available to you. When the experience changes how you feel, chemically, and heightens your attention to the cause, an association will be made. The association will be made in connection to location and time, along with the subject.

That is a prevalent way memories are encoded. As you can see, emotions play a large role. Emotions are engines to act. When you feel anger, you act in rage. When you feel love, you act out of selflessness. This can create a loophole in life because if ignored, much destruction can be done. However, if the loophole is detected and manipulated, it can create a stream of successful events. It is a scientific fact that the brain reacts to and detects patterns. Patterns are the basis of human life because humans are creatures of habit; habits develop from repeated action.

Time should be invested in reflection due to the connection between memory and emotion. The more time you spend reflecting on old memories, new information will turn into wisdom. The infusing of old experiences with new knowledge yields wisdom. Another result of reflection is heightened awareness. Often, memories create patterns that individuals unconsciously seek because of familiarity, even if it is harmful.

An early example persists in childhood trauma. During adolescent years the mind is very impressionable. Anything that a child's mind is exposed to has the chance of affecting their future for an extended period. You will see this happen with love over and over again. Children who grow up in abusive households frequently seek the same environmental conditions out of familiarity, although it is not healthy.

Love is just one example of how patterns developed from the past can take over decision making. When you begin to travel through old experiences, a realization occurs. You will learn what affected you the most, allowing you to make constructive changes. Pattern recognition is nothing more than matching a physical reality with neural networks in your brain. This process is automatic, without your awareness, but can be manipulated for desired effects.

The memory faculty is heavily influenced by emotions. Emotions are engines to act. Actions create habits through repetition. As you learn more information, it will become instinctual to connect information to old and new experiences. Experiences are the foundation of memory creation and habit formation. How can this be beneficial to learn?

When a thought is created, a material equal will form in your environment. Through the law of habit, a thought will crystallize and become a part of who you are. Instead of allowing your thoughts to exist without purpose or concentration, use the law of habit to work for you, not against you. In the brain, a habit is a neural path that has been traveled over many times.

The law of habit can be used to your advantage after learning that fact. Find something that you enjoy enough to spend hours learning about it. Simple exposure will begin to form a neural pathway and remove old irrelevant ones. Each time the action is performed, the path becomes deeper and wider, which engrains the habit in your subconscious mind. Have you ever heard of the phrase practice makes permanent, not perfect?

Practice is a repetitive tool needed to learn any task. People assume that masters are perfect, but that is far from the truth. Masters are nothing more than extraordinary creatures of habit. Perfection is only a concept. The concept of what perfection is grows as you evolve your state of being. Instead of being perfect, masters use science to engrain a specific task, field, or idea into their nervous system.

Science plays a role in calculated evolution. Calculated evolution is the ability to expedite your growth strategically. Elite athletes use scientific formulas to improve their jump shot, run faster, get stronger, or further throw a football. Another group of people who benefit from this science is actors. Actors use science to memorize scripts, manipulate their emotions, and enter different states of mind.

As you can see, it does not matter where you are on the spectrum; science can significantly improve your skillset, especially when it comes to habit formation. Habits are created by repetition and formed under natural law. Your brain will always decide to take the path of least resistance. After the cementation of a thought or action occurs, it will be harder for you to resist the desire versus choosing to engage. Why do you think it is so hard to rid yourself of an addiction?

Now you must understand how to consciously form habits. The environment plays one of the most extensive roles in this process. Your environment not only reacts but produces. Your habits influence the situations and environments that you find yourself in. From the other side, whatever your environment consists of will influence the habits that you form. In turn, producing physical outcomes and situations. Both habit and habitat rely on each other, but you can become conscious of this and use your power to alter your inner mind and future reality.

The stimulus around you acts as a mental feeding ground. With or without your awareness, your mind internalizes what it consumes. This book was designed to make your mind more aware and pick up on the things that are entering your mind daily. Awareness activates power and control. When you become aware of the mechanisms that influence your mind power, it gives you the control to determine your reality. What does environment technically consist of?

Your environment consists of the books you read, the society you live in, your friends, career, country, the clothes you wear, the music you listen to, and the religion you practice, for example. Many elements play a role in your conditioning, thinking, and acting. It is impossible to control every aspect of your environment, but consciousness breeds control, and control is the foundation of power.

Once you develop the ability to concentrate with intensity, your reality will begin to shift, which will play a direct role in your environment. A shift in reality often comes with new friends, ideas, homes, careers, and other life-changing events that help you evolve. Your environment can be controlled through thought concentration. Want a bigger house? Want new friends? Want to make more money?

The key is to develop concentration through practice, meditation, and other activities that require intense focus. What can concentration be compared to? Think of the act of concentrating as the glue that molds laws, practices, and thoughts to build the structure of your brain. Your brain's structure can be translated into the specific areas that stand out and come naturally to you.

What holds the structure together is the foundation. What can the foundation be quantified as? The foundation consists of your daily thoughts, habits, and environments. A weak foundation leads to a broken structure. A broken structure leads to a collapse, which will require rebuilding. The problem occurs when individuals wait until the structure collapses to make changes or become aware. Remember, awareness is one of your most powerful assets because it breeds control. With awareness, you can prevent the structure from collision by being proactive and building a strong foundation in the beginning.

Athletes build a strong foundation by acquiring the correct mindset. As an athlete, you must see yourself as the best. Whether you are the best or not, merely believing you are the best, then making actions that insinuate you are the best translates to becoming the best. As you can see, it starts with belief, which is thought, making thought the foundation of greatness. The second step is action. Action can be considered practice. Practice can be translated into conscious action to develop skills in a concentrated manner.

Without the ability to concentrate your mental forces, power will never be achieved. Some tools allow you to increase concentrative abilities, like meditation. The practice of meditating is used by some elite individuals because it forces them to concentrate on the present moment, which vastly improves awareness. The greatest individual in every field uses repetition to engrain skills into their subconscious to become more unconscious.

Many people will wonder about the precise use of the words unconscious and subconscious. Many people use the words interchangeably, but you must understand the difference between the two regarding scientific mental strategies. When it comes to learning, there are four stages, which allow you to program any skill. It is common for individuals to become great at something but not even know what type of transformation the mind must undergo. In the 1970s, researchers from Gordon Training International improved a theory called the four stages of learning new skills.

Some people are naturally great but can become greater through science. The four stages of learning theorize the process that people go through to learn something new. The power comes when this formula is manipulated and consciously used to elevate in a particular field, which is what the world's best athletes do. People do not understand what goes on in athletes' minds. There is not much luck involved once elite levels are reached. It is not the skill set that separates, but the level of mental awareness, and that does not apply to only athletes but all masters, such as doctors, artists, pilots, truck drivers, hairstylists, investors, and other individuals who are masters of a craft.

The first phase of learning a new skill is called unconscious incompetence. During this phase, you do not understand how to do something because you do not recognize it, and it is unfamiliar. Once you develop value and appreciation for the skill, you can move to the next stage, conscious incompetence. The second stage may consist of many mistakes because simple tasks will require conscious thought. The lack of exposure will lead to mistakes, but mistakes will build on intuitive action.

The result of increased intuition leads you to the third step. You will transition from barely understanding to fully understanding your capabilities, strengths, weaknesses, and averages during this period. Once you understand what you are, it will help you be more precise with your concentration and practice. Increased precision leads to fewer errors and greater results. The last stage of learning is the fourth, where unconscious competence takes control. In the fourth stage, the number 10,000 comes into play.

Masters are masters because the number of hours practiced transformed a once unfamiliar task into something that has become second nature. Unconscious deals with action, while subconscious deals with awareness. Noise can be in the background; while you are not consciously aware, it still enters your subconscious mind. There is no action attached. When you are unconsciously engaged, you are performing a task.

The better you become at something, the more it becomes unconscious, and you can use your conscious mind to focus on higher aspects of the task. As a result, the skill can be performed while executing another task. The individual may teach it to others, depending upon how and when it was learned. The key take away of learning is that you want to become aware and learn how to train your brain.

Your ability to train your memory or develop a skill is a matter of being able to focus. When more hours are spent practicing a given subject, the outline of that subject will be thoroughly impressed upon your mind. The basic fundamentals for learning results in your understanding of attention and how to concentrate it. Anything that is the subject of your attention, whether implicit or explicit, can be referred to as attentional capture.

Without attentional capture, you cannot program your mind consciously. The difference in where attention is placed suggests why two people living the same experience will have two different memories. Attentional capture varies from person to person, which is why perception is important to maneuvering in life.

The difference between implicit and explicit is basically the awareness that you have of the stimulus. Explicit attentional capture happens when something out of focus becomes the focus. An example would be someone calling your name while engaged in a task. Hearing your name would suddenly catch your attention and shift your focus.

In contrast, implicit attentional capture happens when a stimulus affects you, even without your awareness. An example of this could be the long-term conditioning of your environment. Someone born into poverty has a higher chance of committing crimes than someone born into wealth. Seeing crime, drugs, and hopelessness implicitly conditions a subject to learn illegal methods to survive.

The mind does not have to be in focus for you to learn. As long as your mind captures a subject, it has the potential to create connections and pathways in your brain. The understanding of concentration and attention allows you to gain a certain control of your life. As you learn more about your memory, it will be apparent that the mind is nothing more than a machine.

What's so special about the mind is that it collects everything that it is exposed to. Data enters your mind, gets encoded into the subconscious by associating and connecting to neural networks for later retrieval. Elite individuals understand what functions of the mind advance them. The greater your ability to store information becomes, your skillset will enhance. Skills are greatly affected by memory because of the encoding that takes place. First, what is the role of memory?

Memory is the ability to remember past experiences and is a record of the learning process. The human brain has the ability, known as neuro-plasticity, to form new neural pathways, alter existing connections, and adapt and react, affecting how you learn.

How many hours have you spent learning how to properly use this faculty of the mind? In the previous chapters, you learned that intelligence is closely connected to information, recall, and consumption. If memory is responsible for encoding, storing, and recalling information, this natural introduction will exponentially enhance intelligence. Without memories, it would be impossible to learn from experiences or develop relationships. One of the most essential steps to growth resides in reflection.

As you reflect on old experiences, actions can be reevaluated for future correction. When this happens, you can alter your mind to have a different reaction in the future if necessary. There are some cases where you may want to repeat an action, so future results will be the same as past results. A group of individuals who use this method is athletes. Athletes have been referenced a lot because the algorithm translates so well.

When an athlete observes the result of an action, they can choose to repeat the action or manipulate it for a different result. Once the desired result is achieved, the action that created the effect can be repeated repeatedly. For instance, a great basketball shooter makes thousands of jump shots per day. A great pitcher throws thousands of pitches per week. The basis of memory is learning through a process called encoding. Memories are converted into something known as a construct, which contains beliefs and perceptions of reality. Once constructs are created, patterns are then chosen and attracted.

Take an athlete who has negative memories based around a specific moment. Sports are extremely competitive, meaning there are many clutch moments that players must know how to succeed. Clutch moments are moments where pressure is placed on a team and or individual because the room for mistakes is small, and the wrong play can ruin chances of winning. Some athletes perform negatively in these situations due to a construct that was formed based on bad memories.

If a person allows a construct to form, it can take years before it is realized and destroyed. Memories of humiliation can lead to a construct being created. When the construct is formed, a gravitational force will shift this person's mind. The shift literally activates a different person within, who commits unconscious actions, crystalizing the familiar pattern. If the familiar pattern is shame, guilt, or embarrassment, emotions will initiate thoughts, leading to actions that build that construct in the immediate reality.

Patterns and constructs are so powerful that people become prisoners of the same result. This means that a loser will always find a way to lose, no matter what the situation is. On the opposite side of the coin, there are winners. Winners always find a way to come out on top, even if they appear defeated, at some point in the journey. The most important take away is knowing how precisely you can control your mind's functioning without ever seeing the actual wiring or firing with your physical eyes.

The more automatic you can make positive decisions, the less you have to think through life. Your mind is designed to operate like a well-oiled machine. Once you understand that most of your day to day functions are done without conscious thought, it unleashes a spiritual power. A force will guide you in a direction that will evolve you once intuition and faith consume you.

Take some time to think about all the simple things you do daily. The truth is that they may seem simple but are very complex in your mind. Through repetition and exposure, the task becomes so easy, which initiates an autopilot mode. In this mode, your mind may travel to the past or future while still performing the function flawlessly.

Wherever attention goes, energy flows. Whenever your attention is going into the past or entering the future, energy is flowing away from you. The elite individuals and masters of the world know how to use this law for their benefit. As you spend more time learning something, functions become more unconscious, allowing you to focus on higher aspects of the task. Two tennis players can be on the same court but perceive two different matches. One player can be so mentally advanced that more functions are unconscious.

When more functions are unconscious, energy attention can be placed on the present. What this leads to is an ability to focus on an intense amount of energy. This example does not only apply to athletes but anyone competent in a skill. Two people can be competent in the same field but perceive the information and data at two completely different levels. Do not allow your energy to flow away from you, command the present moment, and increase your focus.

Learn to fix your attention on a specific subject. Once this is done at will, for long periods, a doorway will appear. This secret path will lead you to power and prosperity. It should now be clear how much the mind resembles a complex machine. The entire mind is a unit of energy. Within the unit are smaller subsets that play a role in the total operation. As these systems are consciously influenced, there will be an overall increase in power. When power is exercised, it brings forth the creation of material equals.

The simple way to exercise power is through concentration, which has been emphasized as nothing more than focused attention. Through focused attention, you can carve neural paths consciously. To take advantage of this law, you must find something natural to you.

For the athlete, this is their sport. For the scientist, this is their concentration. For the artist, this is their craft. Go back through your memories if you are having trouble finding a natural talent. Your memories are fountains of wisdom that transcends the data in your mind.

The encoding process is a part of all humans. Now that you have the science enhancing, your skillset will be second nature. Once your conscious mind is exposed to the truth, there is no undoing the carved mental path. To achieve the status of elite, you must not only master a field but become so adept at the skill that no one can do what you do better than you. When the spiritual is combined with science, there is no limit to what can be achieved.

With these psychological laws and practices, nothing should be a limitation. A detailed overview of the mind was presented. This information has entered your mind as data. It will be encoded into your memory for later retrieval and activation. Through association and application, the data will exit your mind as an experience or material equal.

What will happen is growth in mindset. The development will transpire due to an enhancement of perspective. As you can see more, your mind will learn how to associate certain bits of information, encode memory, or connect with memories. Naturally, without effort, the way your mind functions will transform over time. It will not be noticed right away but over a period of time. The build of energy will lead to what is considered a blowup.

The process of change is not easy. Sometimes change goes against beliefs and ways of life. Becoming an elite being is not hard but easy when persistent and consistent. The mind is not always explained, but now you have all of the information you need to become elite. There is nothing in between you and greatness but your mind. Take these keys, go to the stars, and never come back.

Part 7

Superconscious Awakening

Part Seven is the pinnacle of the structure that has been built. Depending on where you are in life, this information will have different meanings. There will be people who understand how to utilize this tool on the first encounter. For others, it may take multiple times. Then some will need to encounter some trial and error to truly understand what these words represent. Imagine this message as a device and this book as the instruction manual.

What you will now learn was saved for the end. The instructions will divert from habits and skill development to the highest aspect of perceiving human life. The overall result will transcend you from human to supernatural. The powers which you will develop are mystical in the material world. Think of this as secret teachings for all ages of life.

Part seven is where the dichotomy begins. To properly consume what you are receiving, it must also be applied. Dormant information is as useful as buried jewels. While it may have worth, it does not hold power because it has not been put into circulation. Furthermore, what you consume must be activated.

What you will notice is that the science of your mind is law. It does not matter what generation these laws are utilized; they will always produce the same result. Laws are bound to nature, meaning your forces will always produce a specific outcome when energy is polarized consciously. The foundation began with the layers of the mind, leading to habit formation. The structure was expanded by explaining skill development and exact formulas to mental programming.

It should be clear how to use concentration and attention. The act of concentrating your mental forces is the key to manifesting any internal desire. The transition happens when you transcend outside of your mind to the consciousness of your conscious. To become conscious of consciousness is an ability only available to the rare few. Once your third eye awakens, a different ability is accessed. Slowly, your reality will form around the invisible ideas and inclinations that arise through intuitive action.

In short, there is an invisible world around you. Senses allow you to access reality, but reality is not real. If humans had a different combination of senses, then your experiences in this world would be completely different. Part seven is no longer about your mind but now expanding to the universe.

Prepare your mind by realizing that the universe can be symbolized with your body, mind, and the world. Greatness requires different levels of understanding. The deeper you understand the universe, the higher you rise in life. The spirit governing the universe is the same one that exists inside of you. To understand what you are and what is around you is crucial.

For many, they believe that greatness is some unavailable commodity, prohibiting them from elevating. To become the greatest ever, you must believe you are the greatest ever. Skill acquisition and habits were discussed first for multiple reasons. One reason was that it lays a foundation for any person to develop an ability. The second was done to explain that it does not take luck to learn something.

The universe was not discussed much, but it is the key piece to the puzzle. Once the mind is understood, the universe becomes easy to master. You are in control of your life, but it starts with perception. The pinnacle can only be reached from a God's view, which is a virtue. Greatness is not difficult to obtain because it is inside of you, waiting to be activated.

The universe is one large mind and body of energy. Mind is indeed separate from body, while spirit is separate from mind. What soul is to the body, spirit is to the mind.

Spirit rules over mind. Mind rules over soul, and soul rules over body.

Extend outside of your body to awaken the highest observer. Everything in the universe is a part of a higher system. What cells are to the human body, humans are to the universe. The stars are not separate from you; they are a part of you. In fact, stars are your equal.

The body is inside of the spirit. There is a mind outside of your mind. Your spirit rules over your mind. Your mind rules soul, which governs the body. Actions made by the body, along with the invisible vibrations broadcasted from the solar plexus, aka your gut, create the physical reality around you.

The way that you act and think controls everything that you cannot see. What cannot be seen is the true ruler of your reality. Mental stillness is the key to making the universe surrender. Whatever you think, say or do, the universe will obey. The infinite door only appears when you become one with the all.

How do you find the door? First, your vibration must increase, resulting in the heightening of your frequency. Second, you must seek the infinite source with faith. There must be no fear of entering and no desire to turn back. All old ideas and philosophies must be released. You must come back to this information over time because there will be an awakening with additional life experience.

The moment you enter the universal door, an inpouring of esoteric knowledge will transpire. Inside of the infinite mind exists ancient knowledge and wisdom. Now, allow your mind to absorb the symbolization of nature, mankind, animals, and pyramids to the entire universe. When you dissect and disconnect the human body, it transforms from a whole entity to a collection of parts and systems. The same thing happens when you break down success.

From afar, success may seem like something that happens "overnight," but a different realization is made when studied. Success is the result of small achievements combined and the building of energy. One can always separate into two, and two can always become four. Some laws apply to everything around you.

The human body can be symbolized using the solar system, galaxy, and universe. The study of space is one and the same with biology. What exists outside will always exist inside. In fact, you are not separate from the world, nor the universe. The world is not outside of you, but inside of you. Spirit rules over mind. Soul rules over body.

Break down the reality around you, and a revelation will occur. Mind is the manifestation of spirit. Soul is the manifestation of mind. Body is the manifestation of soul. Once you understand the different planes of reality, it will dawn on you.

Rearrange your mind to analyze the true nature of human existence. Imagine yourself as a car engine. From the perspective of the engine, it is in control of how fast the vehicle goes. While that may be true, there is also something in control of the car, which controls the engine. Your body is a vehicle in this reality. The brain may sit inside of the body, but your mind rules over your brain.

Your mind extends beyond matter into energy. Your spirit extends beyond energy into divine oneness. Matter can be destroyed; energy exists forever. Your body is inside of your spirit, while your soul rests inside of your body. You are the entire world. You are the whole universe.

Human energy extends much further than the physical vehicle being rented. In other words, you are not limited to your body. The power is in the endlessness of space, energy, and time. An awakening occurs when you become conscious of your consciousness. When the mind outside of your mind comes alive, that is the spirit. Only the chosen ones will decipher this coded language.

When awakening the observer, a specific type of control and command is bestowed upon you. In this world, you are taught to believe that God is in the heavens, somewhere above. On the other hand, the Devil who lives in hell is somewhere down below. People are taught to pray to the sky above, but what does the create?

The illusion of an outside power source leads people to believe that they are not in control. While the source of power exists on the outside, it comes to life within. God is within. God is not separate from man, but God is man, and man is God. Your ability to become consciously aware of your consciousness bridges the gap from natural to supernatural.

When an individual begins to evaluate the invisible aspects of life, a revelation occurs. The law of divine oneness explains how everything is one and the same. As above, so below. Imagine a cell in the human body. Cells are invisible to the physical eye but can be seen with the right equipment. Humans are made up of trillions of cells. These cells create systems within the body. For example, there is the digestive, respiratory, and nervous systems.

As a whole, the body is one. Beyond the whole, your body is made up of systems, which are constructed by cells. Now, compare cells of the human body to a human being on this earth. In the material world, billions of humans make up hundreds of countries, which contain cities and smaller communities. There are politicians who govern societies.

Cells divide and multiply. Humans procreate. Turn the switch in your mind to see life in a different light. Humans are the equivalent of cells in this world and universe. How cells make up the human body, humans make up this world, which makes up the galaxy and the solar system. In turn, creating the universe. The entire universe is nothing more than a large body of energy and power. If this information is utilized, it will help you control every aspect of life.

Emotions influence what energy you broadcast and receive. The energy that you broadcast controls the reality around you. Emotions create a surge of energy throughout your body, originating in the solar plexus, also known as the gut. The emotions you feel determine the frequency vibrating to and from you.

Many people live in certain mind states due to the enslavement of their emotions. An emotion such as fear broadcasts with a certain frequency, which is picked up by the universe. Habits such as quitting accompany fear, along with emotions like doubt. When you live in fear or doubt, there is also a constant worry, which translates to turning back or not aiming high for goals.

Everything is one and the same but told in different ways. Symbolism is powerful because the same laws which can be applied to the universe can be applied to you, the individual. You are the universe, meaning that all of the universal laws can be used in your reality. There is a law known as polarity.

With the law of polarity, it is stated that every single entity has an opposite pole. In other words, specific emotions live on one spectrum but on different sides. For instance, love is not different than hate, other than the degree and frequency. Everything in the universe has an opposite. Polarity helps control your energy because it awakens you to placement.

When the concept of duality is internalized, it reveals the secret to harmony. If every emotion has an opposite on the same spectrum, then the way to rid yourself of negative energy is by placing your mental forces on the positive spectrum. For instance, the opposite emotion of fear is courage. It is impossible to overcome fear by thinking about what is creating the fear. Instead, focus on overcoming the obstacle, and courage will lead you to a positive destination.

So many people focus their attention on adverse outcomes or low vibrational emotions. The result creates a vibrational force within, attracting a world without.

Experiences and people confirm the emotions broadcasted, whether negative or positive. Take doubt, for example. Doubt lives on a spectrum with confidence. A person who lives in doubt will attract toxic situations, people, and consistently meet failure. Additionally, people who live in fear also meet failure because when things become difficult, they quit.

Another emotion that can be symbolized is hate. When you harbor hatred, a low frequency will radiate from your gut. The frequency of hate will attract negative people, bad experiences, and other emotions, such as anger and pain. When hate takes over the mind, your reality will always form around toxicity and negativity. The point is emotions resonate with the entire world through invisible vibrations from your solar plexus.

Emotions are a response to a specific trigger each one has a particular purpose. There is no joy without experiencing pain.
Anger, fear, envy, guilt, and sadness are the most common negative emotions. As you become self-aware, it will allow you to identify, name, and handle them.

There are laws to this entire universe. For every cause, there is an effect. For every effect, there is a cause. If you put out good energy, then good energy will return to you. It may be true that the brain is inside of your body, but also understand how the mind is outside of the body. The body and the mind are not one; they are separate entities.

Life will begin to shift when different perspectives are adopted. A simple shift to seeing the body as inside the mind can change how you see the world. What you see with your eyes actually happens within you. Although you can reach your arm out and touch something, it does not mean it is outside of you.

Children are taught to believe in the false reality. Brainwashing begins at a young age. By the time society reaches adulthood, most people are white sheep trained to follow the herd. As long as people are hidden from the truth, it allows globalists and capitalists to control mass groups. When people believe that the things outside of them are greater than them, they lose sight of who they really are. And who you really are is the universe.

The creator is inside, outside, and around you. The world, stars, and moon are actually in the palm of your hands. That simple understanding will give you a sacred key. Good things come to those who put in the work. God is nothing more than a strong source of energy, in fact, the highest source of energy.

Many people have their own beliefs. There is no such thing as right and wrong, so belief does not mean fact. The key is to believe in something. As long as you have a foundation of belief, it will always be room for hope. God is the highest power.

Power is energy. Energy has two forms, negative or positive. To rewrite that equation into one sentence is by saying that God is the highest form of positive energy. Would that make the Devil the lowest form of negative energy? The invisible, spiritual world is one that can be hard to understand.

What this manuscript aimed to do, was not convince, rather shed light. It is not expected for everything to be believed nor understood. As long as a seed was planted, then nature will do the rest. At first, new ideologies can be hard to grasp. Experience creates wisdom, while information creates knowledge.

When information is consumed, it enters the brain as knowledge. Once used, an experience will appear in the outside reality, providing you with wisdom. On this road to success, it not about how quickly you can manifest the envisioned reality. There is a process to manifesting, and the one thing that is required is time.

Imagine each action as a brick. When a positive action is made, one brick is laid. Discipline takes a lot of time and effort. Positive Actions are like laying bricks, and your dream is like the castle. After the first few years, it may seem like it's taking forever, but you have to see the process as the success.

There will be a lot of mistakes and negative thoughts. The more actions you take towards your dream, the more bricks are laid. It takes decades to build castles and only a few months to build a house. So you have to ask yourself, *do you want a house or castle?* Once you answer the question, then understand what it takes to achieve the chosen path.

A dream is not just some regular house; it is a castle. If research is done, it will show that some castles take ten years or longer to build. The relationship magnifies the significance of time. Ten years invested can create something that never dies, lasting lifetimes. Every sacrifice that is made creates a positive opposite result that gives you a higher level of knowledge. Applied knowledge is equal to wisdom.

Wisdom is valued because it is not only information. Wisdom is the result of information applied or lived; hence it is the physical representation of the mental data consumed. Imagine the person who smokes versus the one who breathes in the second-hand smoke. There are side effects, but they are much different. One is more dangerous than the other.

Another takeaway is the potential for the second-hand smoker to become the first-hand smoker. In real-life terms, the best way for some people to understand is by first creating a mental image, then connecting it to real-life experiences. What that will do is create connections with key information. The result will bring the information to life in a unique way, also known as an experience.

When someone consumes enough of something, they will begin to translate that into their outside reality. Envision the smoke as information and knowledge. When a person opens their mind to possibility, it becomes an addiction. The addiction takes over their mind, prohibiting them from wanting any less than what they desire. As that need for manifestation grows, so will the intuitive need to act.

Suddenly, your mind will begin to act on ideas that put you one step closer. Possibilities arise when your mind is no longer satisfied with living average. Two things can happen to make someone question their position in life. The first occurs when someone sees, reads, hears, or interacts with someone who has more or accomplished something of a great magnitude. That one experience can make someone readjust their aim in life.

Someone who once only wanted to acquire a four-year degree went on to become a doctor. What about the person who was a sales associate, then became rich and famous within a year? Then you have the stories of those who had tough backgrounds, but through sheer inspiration, they were able to climb to great heights. All it takes is for a seed to be planted.

Intuitive actions begin to emerge when the seed starts to sprout. When you feel something in their heart and soul, it stems from what was created in the imagination. The imagination is manipulated by thoughts, information, and words. What are you feeding your mind? Information will change the way you perceive the world.

Seeds have been planted by consuming this data. The things you detect will shift. What that will lead to is growth. In other words, when you begin to aim for higher goals, what once satisfied you, is no longer sufficient in fueling the drive. Over the years, your mind will become a sponge.

The bank of wisdom that you are now in possession of was created very strategically. Many people stick to one way of seeing things, but trying something new can open their mind to a world. Your mind has been opened to many new worlds, giving you the ability to connect to reality differently. There will not always be time to prepare, only time to react. Positive reactions lead to positive results.

Every new direction is always a blessing because it's all a part of the greater story. Never allow losses to consume you because an L can easily turn into a W. It's not about failures; it is about recoveries. Will you get back up if you fall? How many times are you willing to fail to succeed?

Your vision emulates a seed. What does this mean? Your thoughts, desires, and prayers ground your mentality, shaping your reality. The only way to manifest is by constant watering. Once the vision is received, the universe, God, and your instincts will send you signs. The secret is to not live blind.

Do not be blind to the fact that you must act. Act now. Invest the time, and the stars will align. Many people have a dream, but sometimes they stop watering in the middle of the process. The worst is when they stop when they are just about to finish the race.

You are now closer to finishing the race. Everything you have consumed will arm you with everything need to reach the light. Many people go their whole life, not understanding who or what they are. If you do not take anything from this manuscript, take this one point. You are the GREATEST to ever live; nothing separates you from those at the top, except your self-belief system.

About the Author

Ken Viñales is a 23-year-old researcher with a B.A. in Psychology. Many years have been spent studying the mind and society. In 2019, he began The Rare Few LLC. In the same year, Viñales began independently publishing and distributing books. The first year could be considered a success. When this journey was chosen, it was never about the optics, but more so about the inner desire. Although millions were not reached in the first year, it did not stop Ken Viñales from aiming high. Now on his third book, with thirty being the life goal, Ken shows how powerful science combined with spirituality is. Many years have been dedicated to finding the master key to success, and after manifesting multiple visions, the power will be transferred to the people. As a writer, Ken Viñales understands that it will take some time for people to catch up to his work, but it will happen one day. The most important thing about words is that they never die, which is the work's primary motivation. One day Ken Viñales will no longer be here, but he will leave a voice behind for people to follow and reach prosperity.

Acknowledgments

I just want to thank you, whoever is on the other side of these pages. Each person that I connect with increases the energy around this vision. If you gained anything from this book, please share it with someone you love and visit TheRareFew.com. My gratitude extends beyond this lifetime!

Made in the USA
Monee, IL
10 November 2020